THE EPICUREAN'S

KITCHEN COMPANION

For my wonderful children,
Amy, Tim and Sam

THE EPICUREAN'S
KITCHEN
COMPANION

PENNY SMITH

Paintings and illustrations by
STEPHEN TREBILCOCK

a rathdowne book
ALLEN & UNWIN

About the artist...

Stephen Trebilcock was born in the Adelaide Hills in 1952. He became a full-time painter in 1986 and was the recipient of the Thomas Laird Memorial Art Prize, a travelling scholarship which took him to the Slade School of Art in the UK.

I first encountered Stephen Trebilcock's beautiful paintings in a gallery window in Adelaide. I was captivated by his talent, strength of colour, composition and, of course, the subjects. Still life paintings are a passion of mine. I am proud, delighted and most grateful that Stephen accepted the challenge to illustrate this collection of recipes—the results are wonderful.

© Penny Smith and individual contributors 1994
Paintings and drawings by Stephen Trebilcock

Design and layout by P.A.G.E. Pty Ltd, South Melbourne, 3205, Victoria

First published in 1994

A Rathdowne Book
Allen & Unwin Pty Ltd
9 Atchison Street
St Leonards NSW 2065, Australia

National Library of Australia
cataloguing-in-publication data

Smith, Penny, 1940-
   The epicurean's kitchen companion.

   Includes index.
   ISBN 1 86373 667 0.

   1. Gastronomy. 2. Cookery. 3. Cookery - Miscellanea. I. Title.

641.013

Printed by South Wind Production, Singapore

10 9 8 7 6 5 4 3 2 1

Contents

$\mathcal{I}$NTRODUCTION

IT IS TWENTY YEARS since I produced my first cookbook. How green I was, ignorant of the difficulties writing a book entailed. Perhaps blind faith and the belief in what I wanted to create helped. I certainly learnt a great deal and benefited from the experience enormously. Looking back on my life, I have always tackled challenges head on. Maybe not immediately, but on some reflection I have plunged into unknown territory to find it most rewarding.

Cork, Fork and Ladle, published by Macmillan in 1975, was a collection of recipes gathered from cooks and food enthusiasts around Australia. It turned out to be an epicurean journey spanning many countries and heritages, with people who had adopted Australia as their home sharing their culinary secrets. We gathered recipes from all areas, professional and amateur alike. It was a beautiful book filled with wonderful photographs and I am sorry that I have never produced a follow-up as, since then, the local culinary scene has altered considerably. Traditional chefs trained in Europe used to be the norm. But gradually in Australia amateur chefs began to appear, opening their own restaurants and making a mark on the culinary scene, a phenomenon unheard-of in the traditional food world. In time some were heralded as geniuses and people trekked to sample their efforts, often in the most humble surroundings.

The greater influx of migrants from Europe in the 1950s brought different foods to our doorstep and even more restaurants appeared, serving such wonders as pasta and paella. We started to grow. Whole areas of suburban cities were settled by people of the same cultural background and you could venture out and sample food from another world very close to home. What riches they shared and how much we learned.

In the 70s and 80s restaurants flourished and eating habits altered. Pubs were to be avoided at all costs as the six o'clock swill (the filling of the belly with as much alcohol as possible before six o'clock and the closure of the bar) made hotels unsavoury places for women. Pubs were not regarded as having any cultural significance. We began to drink wine at home with our meals, but it was still forbidden at public schools and students caught drinking faced expulsion.

Chinese restaurants popped up in every country town and were, for many, the only different cultural food experience rural Australia was familiar with. They served their own particular brand of Chinese cooking and, as nobody had experienced the real thing, they were able to develop a special cuisine unknown, I suspect, in China.

From the turn of the century the Chinese grew fresh produce and supported the gold rush towns with fruit and vegetables that literally kept people alive in areas that had never been cultivated before. We owe those early gardeners a great deal. I can still remember our Chinese greengrocer with his horse and cart, pigtail down to his waist, clopping along Toorak Road, weighing his produce on antique scales and assessing the cost with an abacus. But then in those days we had fresh bread and milk delivered daily by horse and cart. I loved riding to school in the Woodmason's Dairy cart listening to stories told by the milkman, who had only three teeth in his head. We woke to the sound of clinking milk bottles in the early hours of the morning and at school recess every child was given a free milk ration to grow strong teeth and bones.

When my mother took lessons in French cooking our perception of good cooking altered. Who could fail to be impressed with chocolate mousse—that heavenly textured concoction I am sure was my first conscious taste of France? Our family never looked back. With five hungry children, Mum had a captive and enthusiastic audience to experiment on and we devoured all she produced. As the demands grew, a string of European cooks moved in to help feed us, and I can well remember food put on our table from Spain, Ukraine, Holland and Italy. Lasagne was totally unfamiliar to me until my teens. As for tropical fruit— pineapples maybe, and bananas, but mango and pawpaw were unknown. Today we have a house in the Far North of Queensland and mangoes and avocadoes grow in the garden in abundance. We take such luxury for granted. But when my grandmother served avocado as an entree at a beautiful dinner dance she gave in the early 60s, very few of the guests knew what they were eating and it was certainly considered an acquired taste.

Today my youngest son Sam will plead with me, 'Why can't we have normal food like other people?' The two eldest children, however, have turned into excellent cooks and Tim now works in the industry—so something rubs off eventually.

After my mother's success with French cookery lessons I persuaded Macmillan to publish the complete collection of Madame de Stoop's recipes, shared by so many during her very successful classes in Melbourne. We called the collection *The Pleasure of the Table* and it was beautifully illustrated by Donald Green.

The following year, late one night while lying awake, I conceived the *Epicurean Diary*. I had already published *Salad in Season*, and my editor, Susan Haynes, had become a good friend and was very receptive to new ideas. Susan supported everything I did and was very enthusiastic about the idea. The first edition was published in 1984 and I continued to compile the diaries until 1993. In researching wherever I went, I collected recipes from ancient books, family archives, restaurateurs and ordinary cooks who shared enthusiasm for good food and its professional execution. Many recipes had been handed down through generations, tested and tried on each new family, and treasured. Such recipes provoke nostalgic thoughts for many, producing a warm glow as we remember times in our lives less complicated and simpler than today.

After ten years we ceased compiling the diaries, and I often look over the richness enclosed in the ten small volumes I have lived with daily. I re-read them now and my thoughts swell to the many happy experiences I lived through collecting the recipes you have before you in this book. So much history, so many special occasions that were times for Grandmother's cake or pudding. During interviews people would talk longingly of Christmas and the family pudding. I have selected several here and they are all excellent—only your special preference will differentiate between them.

I want these recipes to be recorded, for food styles and eating habits are changing almost as fast as technology. Where will all the history go? How will we relate to our past if it all becomes swallowed up on computer disc, in libraries few will visit? Who will care, you might say? Maybe no-one, but just maybe, there will be some enthusiasts of our culture who wish to understand where we came from—that when we poured the tea and sat to share news of joy or grief we baked a cake, that we filled the jar with biscuits, cooked in 44-gallon drums under shady trees for shearers, or ate in restaurants unique to Australia and our own particular heritage. That is how our cuisine evolved, and we enjoyed it all.

You have in your hands, I believe, a very special collection of recipes from all over the country. They were given willingly and I reproduce them with the love and respect they so richly deserve. Included are words penned by friends all active in the food industry who have made a distinctive contribution. They are a learning experience also and a time warp. The words were meant to be shared and I reproduce them because I enjoyed them so and still do. Again, my sincere thanks to all who contributed and I hope everyone who reads what has been written will be the richer for it.

KITCHENS FROM HELL

COOKS AND would-be cooks dream of a culinary nirvana—a stainless steel kingdom where all the knives are Dick and Sabatier and heavy-based copper saucepans never need polishing. The self-cleaning stove in this ideal kitchen has a minimum of two electric ovens (one of course with a convection fan), a char grill that never smokes, and gas burners with more BTUs than a blow-torch.

In addition to the Rosieres or Zanussi is a chilled marble slab for effortless pastry and enough bench space to prepare a meal for a small family gathering of 48. The layout has Zen perfection, with prep-bench, stove and refrigerator forming a 'magic work-triangle' sought by those involved in workplace design.

The myth of the perfect kitchen is alive and well, promoted and fed by glossy magazines and articles—a kitchen of flawless design in which cooking is always easy and trouble-free. Sadly, the myth falls short of reality. Cooking is never effortless and trouble-free, even with well-pedigreed appliances and perfect layout. And for those of us not blessed with a glamorous kitchen, cooking remains a total pain in the arse. We cook with Staysharp knives that are forever blunt, thin aluminium saucepans that stick, and ovens with 'hot spots' and uncalibrated controls guaranteeing burnt offerings and frazzled nerves—hot, constricted places without enough room to swing a chicken. These are the 'Kitchens from Hell', and I've cooked in more than my fair share of them.

The most memorable was hardly a kitchen at all—rather a makeshift collection of pie-warmers, barbecues and portable gas rings assembled to cook a four-course meal for 200 people during the Barossa Vintage Festival. The unventilated area immediately filled with clouds of smoke as we began searing the meat during the afternoon prep session. Conditions were so smoky that the winery's carpenters were summoned to remove the roofing iron from the building. This proved to be an effective but somewhat flawed method of ventilation as it began to rain at the height of service that night. Once again the carpenters were summoned, this time to hammer the roof back on!

Inadequate extraction remains the bane of domestic kitchens. Ordinary fans are OK if you are poaching an egg or warming milk, but completely underpowered for grilling and roasting given that most chefs like to operate at full power. It is virtually impossible to cook 'like the pros' at home without the fire brigade being called by worried neighbours.

Ovens are the most fickle of appliances—a lesson I learnt at a young age on a skiing holiday with Len Evans and family. Boldly I agreed to prepare dessert as part of an ongoing cooking competition and, never one to cook something simple when a complicated dish would do, I chose to bake a classic croquembouche. Using a friend's kitchen, with a small but adequate stove fuelled by a gas bottle on the side of the building, I began my creation. Initially the choux balls rose perfectly, like golden golf balls—only to deflate before my very eyes when the gas ran out. Without fuel to cook another batch or to make the toffee with which to glue the pyramid together, my mind moved into damage-control mode. What I needed was cream and chocolate— cream to fill and reshape the flaccid balls and chocolate to use in place of toffee.

With no ordinary cream to be found, I used sour cream instead. 'Thredbo in Spring'—a hill of non-spherical balls filled with sour cream, tentatively held together by melted chocolate bars—may not have been a taste success, but it remains my own personal triumph over kitchen adversity.

The maxim 'What can go wrong will go wrong' is especially pertinent when cooking for large numbers using small pots and inappropriate storage vessels. Many years ago, my mother cooked cassoulet, that wonderful, hearty peasant dish of beans, pork, mutton, sausage and goose, to be served following a tasting of very old wines. Cooking thirty litres of the stuff in a small domestic kitchen proved no easy task. Once completed, we were to store and transport the cassoulet in a large plastic rubbish bin bought expressly for the task. In our haste we did not allow the mix to cool sufficiently prior to the transfer to the bin. The result was catastrophic. The plastic bin split from its base to its middle, vomiting a lava flow of beans all over the kitchen floor.

Upon reflection, a perfect kitchen may not take the drudgery out of food but it is certainly preferable to cooking in an imperfect one. Now, if only I could trade in the old electric oven on a Paul Bocuse—and move the workbench in the corner to create an equilateral triangle...

Michael Hill Smith, South Australia

OUR KITCHEN
AT MILLSWYN STREET

OUR KITCHEN was where it was at. More than any other room in the large house I lived in as a child, the kitchen summons the most memories and feelings about what was once my home. Our kitchen was a living, breathing thing which was in a constant state of evolution. It would change daily and I would watch with a keen sense of wonder every change, no matter how minute, and marvel at what was the embodiment of my mother's greatest creation.

To think of the kitchen is to think of my mother, for the two could never be separated. I cannot remember a day when she was not in it. Her continued presence made her lord and master of all she surveyed, and we were tolerated at some times and not at others.

The walls of our kitchen witnessed many an ordeal—from family dramas (always numerous in our house) to per-haps the happiest times, when we were all together at the end of the day, content with the security and warmth which comes from loved ones sharing the same uncomplicated space and breaking bread.

Our house revolved around meal times, and therefore the centre of our universe was the kitchen. It represented a most important place, in which 'she who must be obeyed' would spend hours planning and preparing delicious and mysterious arrays of the finest fare to feed our little, growing faces. Mum's gastronomic scope and skills knew no bounds and her culinary genius was aided only by the four walls and an inexhaustible supply of cookware, with which she was most intimate. Each meal she cooked was designed with a specific purpose in mind, and all of us came to look upon this family ritual as a journey with a beginning, a middle and, more often than not, a dreaded end when there was no more left on the plate and we would be faced with the prospect of another day until we could resume the experience.

Everything in our kitchen belonged in a special and unique place and had to be maintained in a certain state, which demanded the ultimate in preservation. 'Wear and tear' was not a concept Mum rated high on her list of Acceptable Normalities, as she cared for every utensil with such ferocious force it put my father's and brothers' efforts to shame. I guess you could say that Mum had a love affair with her kitchen and everything in it. Just like lovers do, she became possessive and distressed when the harmonious state she endeavoured to preserve at all times was disrupted by the event of a broken cup, a chipped knife or the dishwasher left unpacked.

I was probably the most successful at imitating her state of 'perfection' when it came to cleaning the kitchen. The boys seemed to acquire a most selective sort of amnesia with regard to doing things 'properly', and therefore Yours Truly got the job of bettering their feeble efforts before Mum was subjected to the degradation of her most precious space. I did not mind, as it meant more to her than anything in the world to come home and find everything in order just as she had left it.

It's amazing how much of an influence our kitchen had on all our lives. My friends always loved our kitchen because it had a life of its own and they could feel it. It possessed layers and layers of experience which reflected our history as a family. I couldn't imagine ever disassembling it, as a spell would have been broken—but things change and we must change with them.

I have my own kitchen now, and am just beginning the first of the series of 'love affairs' I know I, too, will have with this particular space in my house. It is a sensual place which I will fill with all the good things my husband and I both love—and that makes it special. Sometimes he makes me walk him around our kitchen so he can see it through my eyes and understand the balance I strive for—why, like my mother, I arrange my copper cooking pots a certain way and make sure the handles of my beautiful china cups all point in a certain direction. He says it is amazing that I am so intimate and in tune with my surroundings, and I try to explain the pure joy I derive from placing a fresh bunch of sweet-smelling basil in a certain jug, or the pleasure I feel when I make tea in a special way in my silver teapot and drink the first cup from my treasured bone china.

Perhaps these unexpected and mysterious thrills are what make a kitchen more special than any other room in a house, or maybe kitchens simply have magic of their own. If you're lucky, you too may fall under the spell.

Amy Smith, New South Wales

Soups

BEETROOT SOUP

800 g beetroot
300 ml red wine
pinch of aniseed
100 g butter with a dash of
    oil
1 onion, chopped
2 sticks of celery, chopped
$\frac{1}{2}$ fennel, chopped
2 carrots, cleaned and sliced
100 g cabbage, sliced
fresh thyme
75 ml sour cream

Wash the beetroot and boil half of them in salted water until tender. Peel and shred, and let stand in a bowl with the red wine and aniseed for at least 2 hours.

Peel and slice the rest of the beetroot. Melt the butter and oil in a heavy pan and toss in the raw beetroot and all the vegetables. Add 5-6 cups of water and boil for 30 minutes. Add the thyme halfway through the cooking.

Strain the soup, rescuing enough of the cooking liquid to purée all the vegetables to finish the soup. Reheat the purée and add the marinated beetroot and wine. Check for seasoning. Stir in the sour cream.

Can be served hot or cold.

SERVES 6

Edouard Demaneuf, Victoria

CHESTNUT SOUP

250 g chestnuts
2 onions
1 carrot
1 stick of celery
butter
1.5 litres stock
salt and pepper
sherry
cream

Peel the chestnuts after cutting round the curved side and boiling for a couple of minutes. Take off both the shell and the skin—this requires a bit of a knack, but can be done easily if the chestnuts are still hot.

Melt some butter in a pot. Put the pot on the heat and brown the chopped onion, carrot and celery. Add the chestnuts, seasoning and stock. Cook until the chestnuts are breaking up (about 20 minutes for fresh chestnuts).

Blend in the food processor. Reheat and serve, if you wish, with a little sherry and a dollop of cream.

SERVES 4-6

Jennifer Hillier, South Australia
Derived from Elizabeth David, Italian Food *(1954)*

CHERVIL SOUP

WIVINE DE STOOP brought French haute cuisine within the reach of Australian women. For the first time, the traditional cooking of France was demonstrated in beautiful surroundings with an elegance and expertise rarely matched even today. Here are her thoughts on chervil.

'As far back as I can remember I was always very fond of chervil. On the farm in Belgium we grew this aromatic herb in large beds, as we used it regularly in our soups, in salads and with butter sauces. When I arrived in Australia in 1952, the first thing I was anxious to do was to plant my herb garden. Being able to grow fresh tarragon, chives and chervil was a challenge as they were little-known. As well, I planted cress and purslane, just to name two.

'Chervil originated in Russia and was cultivated from the beginning of the Christian era. It is very easy to grow in Australia. It resembles parsley, with finer, curled, light-green leaves which are delicately flavoured. In Victoria, sow the seeds from September to April in a shady position. This is most important.

'I am aware that we can buy herbs in the best greengroceries, even at the markets, but I still think they will never be as fresh as the ones you pick from your own garden just at the moment you need them.

'Here is a very simple recipe for a soup which has been in our family repertoire for many years and which I still use today.'

15 g butter
60 g onions, sliced
90 g young leeks, sliced
125 g potato, cut into cubes
175 g chervil
salt and pepper
625 ml (2½ cups) chicken stock
100 ml (5 tablespoons) chicken stock, extra

Melt the butter in a pot and add the onions. Allow to soften. Add the leeks and potato and stir well. Add 100 g of the chervil, the salt and pepper, and then the chicken stock.

Bring to the boil and allow to simmer for 20 minutes. Cool and vitamise. Vitamise the remaining chervil with the extra stock and add to the soup just before serving. This allows you to retain all the freshness of the chervil flavour.

SERVES 6-8

Wivine de Stoop, Victoria

Add the avocado pip *to salads or soups containing avocado to prevent discoloration. Remove before serving.*

YABBIE CONSOMMÉ WITH SQUASH BLOSSOMS

HOWQUA DALE Gourmet Retreat in Victoria is famous for its beautiful setting, excellent accommodation and delicious food. Run by Marieke Brugman and Sarah Stegley, it has created an atmosphere of excellence unparalleled in Australia. The following recipe comes from Marieke's kitchen and uses ingredients from the kitchen garden.

Pick your squash blossoms early in the morning before the heat of the day has softened the petals. Remove the stamens from the blossoms and prepare a mousseline filling.

MOUSSELINE FILLING FOR SQUASH BLOSSOMS

300 g raw yabbie flesh obtained from the pincer claws and tails
salt and pepper
few drops lime juice
few drops Cognac
few drops Tabasco
30 g egg white
250–300 ml cream
12 squash blossoms

CONSOMMÉ

heads and shells from 2–3 kg yabbies
1 small carrot, finely chopped
1 leek, finely chopped
1 kg sun-ripened tomatoes, chopped
15 cm vanilla bean, split
1 tablespoon olive oil
350 ml white wine, on the sweet side
1 cup mixed vegetables (carrots, celery, leek, parsley stalks), chopped
1 cup egg white

If your yabbies are alive, plunge them into boiling water for 30 seconds. This will not cook them but allows the meat to come away from the shell easily.

Put the yabbie flesh, with some salt and pepper, the lime juice, Cognac and Tabasco, into the refrigerator to chill for 1 hour. Put your food processor bowl into the freezer for 1 hour.

Remove the bowl and yabbies from the refrigerator and process the yabbies to a paste. Add the egg white and keep processing until the mixture is smooth and glossy. Add the cream.

Transfer the mousseline to a piping bag with a wide nozzle. This can be done up to 24 hours ahead and left to chill in the refrigerator.

Pipe the mixture evenly into your blossoms and steam in a Chinese bamboo basket set over boiling water with the lid on. Check after 5 minutes. Don't steam too vigorously or for too long, or the mousseline will split.

Thoroughly clean out the insides of the yabbie heads. Break heads, claws and shells up with a mallet or in batches in the food processor. Heat oil in a large stockpot and sauté the shells until well coloured. Add the vegetables and stir until they take on an aroma. Deglaze with the wine, cover with cold water and add the vanilla bean. Simmer steadily for 1 hour or more, skimming the surface regularly until you have a well-flavoured broth. Strain, pushing on the solids to extract all their flavour, and refrigerate overnight.

Next day, clarify the broth: In a food processor, make a paste from the cup of vegetables and the egg white. Remove any fat from the broth and whisk the vegetable/egg white mixture into the cold broth. Continue to whisk over heat until the mixture comes to the boil. Simmer on very low heat for 1 hour.

Carefully remove the crust that has formed and ladle the clear consommé into a double layer of wet muslin to strain. Steam the squash blossoms and put them into warm soup bowls. Reheat the consommé and ladle over the blossoms. Serve.

SERVES 6

Marieke Brugman, Victoria

SWEET POTATO AND CORIANDER SOUP

750 g sweet potato
250 g potato
60 g butter
2 cloves garlic
1 cup coriander, chopped
(including scrubbed roots
and stems)
1 tablespoon fresh ginger,
finely chopped
500 ml chicken stock
1 cup cream
salt and pepper to taste
extra coriander to serve

Peel and cut the potato into 2 cm pieces. Steam briefly and dry. Melt the butter in a pan and sauté the potato, garlic, coriander and ginger. Pour on the stock and bring to the boil. Simmer for 10 minutes and allow to cool. Purée the mixture in a blender, add the cream and season to taste.

For a more elegant presentation, force the cooked potato through a mouli légume. Use only half a cup of cream and, when serving, pour the soup over a spoonful of crème fraîche in the bowl, then garnish with coriander leaves.

SERVES 6

David Hay, South Australia

Remove the stalk *end only from beans, not the tip—it is full of extra vitamins.*

◇ ◇ ◇ NOTES ◇ ◇ ◇

When boiling potatoes, *add a pinch of sugar as well as salt to make them dry and floury when cooked.*

Salads

WHEN IS A SALAD NOT A SALAD?

THESE DAYS this may seem a difficult question to answer. A salad, says Larousse, is a dish made up of herbs, plants, vegetables, eggs, meat and fish seasoned with oil, vinegar, salt and pepper, with or without other ingredients. It would be hard to improve on that definition which does, after all, leave ample room for the creative cook to indulge in personal originality.

Visiting America recently I discovered there that a salad was a very different dish to the satisfying side salad we have come to expect in Australia, a mixture of fresh greens coated with a delicate vinaigrette. On the American menu, the salad course may be described as a Caesar Salad with Thousand Island Dressing. Once you decipher the terminology you will find that the salad is almost always a mountain of ingredients completely coated with a bottled prepa-ration that disguises and overpowers the wilted bits and pieces it dresses. Salads in America and Canada even accompany sandwiches, and fight for space on high platters with equally large obligatory piles of chips or 'fries'. Very rarely did I receive that refreshing mélange of green leaves with its subtle preparation of good-quality vinegar and oil. The Sooke Harbour House on Vancouver Island was an exception. It served the prettiest salads I have ever seen. Properly dressed with their own vinaigrettes, delicate leaves of varietal lettuce grown on the premises were colourfully garnished with flower petals from the restaurant garden picked minutes before service. They looked almost too good to eat.

A salad need not be complicated to be good. Freshness and care in the quality of the ingredients is of the utmost importance. A salad should refresh the

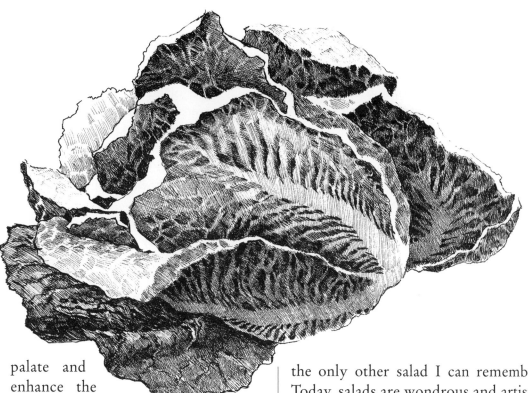

palate and enhance the meal, aid the digestion and appeal to all the senses.

When asked to write a book on salads some years ago, I thought it an impossible task. When I got going, though, I found it difficult to stop. The combinations seemed endless. I found this interesting, as the salads of my youth consisted largely of the good old Aussie concoction of grated carrot, sliced tinned beetroot and cubes of cheddar thrown in on top of an iceberg lettuce. Coleslaw is the only other salad I can remember. Today, salads are wondrous and artistic creations that have become an important part of the complete meal. We have introduced the salad as a main course more frequently and as summer approaches you may need a little more inspiration, so here are a few unusual salads to try.

Penny Smith, Victoria

PAT BLAKE'S CAESAR SALAD

ONE SUMMER holiday I was staying at French Island with friends. Colonies of wild birds had nested and their chicks had hatched. It was very hot this summer, and on one of those rare, magical days you never forget we tried swimming in the dam to cool down. The mud caked and cracked on our bodies as we climbed up the bank to dry. We drifted back to the house to quench our thirst. It was too hot to prepare anything for lunch.

Towards afternoon the sky, usually dungaree blue, was leached of colour. As the temperature pushed up to 45 degrees the landscape seemed to lift above the horizon and float gently as if on another universe. We were without motivation, and yet the sacred ibis on the island were congregating on the swamp at the water's edge. Every now and then a rush of wings could be heard as they were joined by more of their kind.

At 5.00 pm the rooster crowed continuously , as if it were dawn, in protest at the heat. But his hens were nowhere to be seen. The earth baked and baked, biscuit-dry, and we waited for dusk. We had tried to lie on our beds but the sheets had felt scorched as the sun poured liquid heat onto the tin roof. All the occupants of the farmhouse cooked in their own particular agony, and the wind howled from the north making the house feel like an oven.

Outside, the swans sat on the foreshore in the blazing sun—fortunate creatures they, who could immerse their bodies into the abyss of seaweed and grey silt. Pelican chicks, many on their nests and still naked of feathers, ventilated frantically to stay alive. I walked out to check how they were coping and the parent birds flew off as I approached, disgorging fish which quickly stank in the heat, for their young. I too was hungry, and preparing meals was my contribution to the holiday. I could think of nothing more palatable than a Caesar salad a friend had prepared for me on another very hot day during summer in the Canadian Rockies. I have used this recipe many times with great success. All the ingredients are cupboard staples—you just need to buy a good, fresh lettuce.

1½ cups corn oil
½ cup lemon juice
2 cloves garlic
1 egg
1 small can anchovies in oil
4-5 drops tabasco or
  Worcestershire sauce to
  taste
4 slices stale bread
1 romaine (cos) lettuce
2 tablespoons freshly grated
  parmesan

Combine half a cup of the corn oil, lemon juice, garlic, egg, anchovies and oil in the blender with the tabasco or Worcestershire. Cut the bread slices into cubes and deep-fry in one cup of oil until golden. Drain on brown paper. Wash and dry the lettuce. Break it into small pieces and put it into a serving bowl. Scatter on the croûtons and pour on enough of the prepared dressing to coat the salad. Scatter on the parmesan before serving.

SERVES 4

Penny Smith, Victoria

CRAYFISH SALAD WITH NASTURTIUM FLOWERS

1 whole crayfish, cooked
100 g mixed salad greens
1 small bunch rocket
200 g snake beans
nasturtium flowers, buds
    and leaves
2 teaspoons French
    wholegrain mustard
2 teaspoons sugar
1 small red chilli
1/3 cup white wine vinegar
1 cup peanut oil
salt and pepper

Remove the crayfish meat from the shell and prepare 6 equal portions. Set aside. Wash the salad greens, beans and nasturtiums. Portion them onto each plate. Place the crayfish pieces on top, and prepare the dressing.

Split the chilli, remove and discard the seeds, and chop finely. Put the mustard into a jar with the sugar, salt and pepper. Pour in the vinegar, add the chilli and oil. Shake well. Spoon liberally over the salad and serve.

SERVES 6

Anita Hughes, Victoria

PICKLED VEGETABLE SALAD

To ACCOMPANY raw tuna, venison and game birds.

peeled tasty pumpkin
1 leek
2 carrots
4 spring onions
8 Chinese mushrooms,
    soaked in warm water for
    an hour and squeezed dry

DRESSING
3 tablespoons sugar
250 ml (1 cup) white wine
    vinegar
250 ml (1 cup) water

Prepare a very fine julienne of the vegetables and combine in a bowl.

Dressing: In a pan dissolve the sugar in the vinegar by stirring over heat. Add the water and reduce the liquid by half. Pour, while still hot, over the prepared vegetables. Mix thoroughly and cover with plastic wrap. Allow to stand for 30 minutes before serving.

SERVES 4

Klaus Lemm, Victoria

To store lettuce, *separate the leaves and soak in cold water for 30 minutes, dry in a salad spinner, fold in a clean tea-towel and store in the refrigerator crisper.*

PINK GRAPEFRUIT AND POMEGRANATE SALAD

2 pink grapefruit
2 pomegranates
1-2 tablespoons castor sugar

Segment the grapefruit and put in a bowl. Take one pomegranate and roll it backwards and forwards on the table to crush the seeds inside. Press the skin with your fingers. When the pomegranate feels quite soft inside, pierce a small hole in the side and squeeze out as much juice as possible into the bowl. Cut the pomegranate in half and scoop out the seeds into a nylon sieve. Press any remaining juice over the grapefruit.

Cut the other pomegranate in half and carefully remove the seeds, clearing them of all white pith. Put them into the bowl with the grapefruit. Sprinkle with sugar and taste for sweetness. Leave to macerate for at least an hour.

Serve chilled, in pretty white bowls on plates. Garnish with mint or lemon balm leaves.

SERVES 4

Darina Allen, Ireland

WILTED LETTUCE SALAD

THIS SALAD is a simple and delicious concoction I was served in a log cabin high in the Canadian Rockies one summer.

2 iceberg lettuces
6 rashers bacon
salt and pepper
pinch sugar
2 tablespoons vinegar
chive flowers

Chop the lettuce into bite-sized pieces and put them into a serving bowl. Sprinkle on the salt, pepper and sugar. Fry the bacon rashers until very crisp. Drain and crumble. Pour off all but 3 tablespoons of the bacon fat from the pan and add the vinegar. While still hot, pour this over the lettuce and serve immediately. Garnish with chive flowers.

SERVES 6

Norma Blake, Canada

SPECIAL SALAD DRESSING

JUDY CRITTENDEN'S husband Doug and son Brett were well-known wine merchants in Victoria and New South Wales. Judy has an extensive vegetable garden in Melbourne where she grows a large range of culinary plants as well as many varieties of lettuce. She sows her lettuce seeds all year round. The seeds are planted a few at a time and well spaced, directly into the garden bed. Seedlings that grow too close together are transplanted.

In summer Judy plants predominantly the green and brown mignonette, and the non-hearting Regency (Yates) which is a large, claret-red leafed lettuce that needs plenty of space. The Narromar variety, with its crunchy leaf and frilly edge, can be planted in summer and winter. In winter cos is a good grower (it does not do so well in summer), as are endive and chicory. Italian varieties should be planted in autumn as they become too bitter in the heat of summer.

When the lettuces have developed leaves 5 cm in size, begin picking from the outside. Take a few from each plant—then you won't have the problem of them all being ready at the same time, and the lettuces will stay small and tender and without a tough heart.

Seed beds are prepared by digging in compost 10 cm deep. Judy's compost is made from scraps from her kitchen and garden.

COMPOST
Combine 2 buckets soft green vegetable matter including citrus, 1 bucket hard green material such as twigs, and 1/2 bucket fowl or sheep manure or 1/4 bucket dynamic lifter or seaweed. Turn the mixture every 3 days. Damp it down and cover with plastic, keeping it loose and aerated. In summer it is usable in 3 weeks, but it takes longer in winter. Sit your seedlings on top of the plastic: the heat generated from the compost ensures they are kept warm and frost-free.

SPECIAL SALAD DRESSING
1 rounded dessertspoon
   Dijon mustard
1 level dessertspoon sugar
65 ml (1/4 cup) French
   tarragon vinegar
65 ml (1/4 cup) Nove brand
   gherkin juice
3 dessertspoons Master Foods
   dried salad herbs
1 heaped dessertspoon dried
   basil

Combine all ingredients in a large jar and allow to stand to soften the dried herbs. Then add the following:
   125 ml (1/2 cup) extra light olive oil
   125 ml (1/2 cup) sunflower oil
   1/2 teaspoon oriental sesame seed oil
   a good pinch seasoned pepper (McCormicks)

Using as many different lettuce leaves as you can, add slices of red pepper and avocado with thinly sliced Italian tomatoes in oil, parsley and chervil. To finish the salad after tossing in the dressing, drizzle on a teaspoon of oil from the tomatoes just before serving.

Judy Crittenden, Victoria

SPINACH SALAD WITH MAGENTA EGGS

THE EGGS must be prepared at least three days in advance.

12 very small fresh eggs
(pullet eggs)
1 bunch baby beets
2 tablespoons sugar
1 level teaspoon salt
1 cup red wine vinegar

Prick the base of each egg and drop them carefully into boiling water to hard-boil for 8 minutes. Stir at the beginning to centre the yolks. Chill in cold water and peel.

Remove the leaves and most of the stalks from the beets. Cook the beets in boiling water to just cover until just tender. Strain the cooking liquid through muslin and reserve, allowing it to cool.

Peel the beets and put them into a jar with the peeled eggs. Add the sugar and salt. Pour in the vinegar and top the jar with beet juice, making sure the beets and eggs are covered. Seal and refrigerate until ready to use.

VINAIGRETTE
2 tablespoons red wine
vinegar
8 tablespoons olive oil
salt and pepper to taste
pinch sugar

Vinaigrette: Shake all ingredients until blended.

SALAD
150 g baby spinach leaves
1 butter lettuce
2 small red witlof
12 magenta pickled eggs
1 avocado
200 g ham pieces
½ cup pinenuts
purple basil if available

Salad: Wash the spinach and lettuce thoroughly and spin dry. Arrange on a platter. Cut the base from the witlof and arrange on top of the lettuce. Cut the eggs into quarters and slice the avocado into wedges, then arrange on top of the salad.

Cut the ham into small dice. Fry until crisp and toss over the salad. Roast the pinenuts until golden and add just before serving. Shred the basil and scatter on. Pour over the vinaigrette.

SERVES 6

Penny Smith, Victoria

SUMMER WITLOF

SUMMER in our house at Eildon in Victoria was always relaxed and casual. I used to sit on the top of our ridge and watch in peace as evening approached and the sun bathed the distant hills in a dust-like veil, softening the ridges and valleys and making them appear mystical. The swallows, like pointed darts, swooped in the tepid breeze collecting hapless insects left drunk by the warmth and haze. Often at dusk the raucous cry of the cockatoo shattered the stillness and the distant laugh of a kookaburra heralded the approaching night. And the sun sank. I have seen no grander canvas, no spectacle to match that three-dimensional splendour.

Today there is a lonely cloud, a single puff of white. It promises little as the temperature holds and we lounge, languid and bathed in sweat, awaiting the dark. As the shadows lengthen I have to move indoors. The mosquitoes, vigorous in the night, swarm to prey on new blood, any blood. I resent their intrusion into my world.

It is time to go in and prepare the evening meal. A witlof salad with grapes and cress, tiny shavings of raw onion, blanched walnuts to give it texture, and a creamy dressing is all I can enjoy.

6 yellow and, if possible, red
    witlof
sultana grapes
1 small onion
1/2 cup walnut pieces (fresh
    from the shell)
fresh land or water cress

Separate the witlof leaves. Pick the grapes from their stems and cut in half. Cut the onion very thin on a mandolin. Blanch the walnut pieces in boiling water. Peel them and roast in the oven until golden. Combine all ingredients in a serving bowl.

DRESSING

2 teaspoons sherry vinegar
    (I use the one made by
    Yalumba)
4 tablespoons olive oil
1 tablespoon orange juice
1 teaspoon Dijon mustard
1/2 teaspoon sugar
good pinch salt
freshly ground pepper

Mix all ingredients together in a bowl and drizzle over salad before serving.

SERVES 4

Penny Smith, Victoria

Do not wash witlof—*washing with water increases the bitterness and causes discoloration. Discard the outer leaves and wipe with a damp cloth. In other countries witlof is also referred to as Belgian endive and chicory.*

◇ ◇ ◇ NOTES ◇ ◇ ◇

Keep onions *in the refrigerator for 24 hours*
before slicing—it helps reduce tears.

Vegetables & Pasta

ASPARAGUS RISOTTO

1 medium-sized onion,
  finely chopped
2 tablespoons olive oil
500 g Arborio rice
1.5 litres chicken stock
1 kg asparagus, cut into
  1 cm pieces
salt and freshly ground
black pepper
100 g butter
100 g parmesan, grated

Sauté the onions in the oil. Add the rice and sauté for 2 minutes, stirring continuously. Add a ladle of stock and stir until it is all absorbed. Add asparagus, seasonings and another ladle of broth. Keep stirring and adding stock, ladle by ladle, until rice is cooked. Take off the heat and stir in butter and parmesan. Serve immediately.

SERVES 6-8

Bill Marchetti, Victoria

CARROT AND NUTMEG TART

250 g shortcrust pastry

FILLING
100 g finely grated carrot
60 g ground almonds
2 egg yolks
1 egg white
150 ml cream
60 ml melted, cooled butter
1/2 teaspoon nutmeg, freshly
  ground
2 tablespoons castor sugar

Preheat the oven to 200°C. Line a 22 cm flan tin with shortcrust pastry, fill with crumpled foil and dried beans. Bake blind for 15 minutes until quite cooked and pale brown. Remove from oven and lower oven to 180°C.

Filling: Mix all ingredients for filling together. Taste to see if there is enough sugar for your taste. Remove foil and beans and pour filling into shell. Bake at 180°C for 15-20 minutes until the filling has set and has developed a golden crust. Serve warm or cold.

SERVES 6

Stephanie Alexander, Victoria
Adapted from a recipe of Hannah Glasse

When boiling vegetables *30-40 per cent of their mineral content is lost in the water. They also lose certain vitamins through heat, so it's better to cook them less or eat them raw.*

ASPARAGUS SOUFFLÉ

1 kg asparagus
125 g butter
125 g flour
2 tablespoons freshly grated
   parmesan
pinch cayenne
4 egg yolks
5 egg whites
pinch salt
milk

Cut the tips from the asparagus stalks and set aside. Peel and cook the stalks until just tender. Drain and reserve liquid.

Butter and crumb a large gratin dish. Melt the butter in a double boiler and stir in the flour until smooth. Add a mixture of 3 parts milk and enough asparagus cooking liquid to equal 1 litre (4 cups) of liquid, or until the sauce is the consistency of thin cream. Cook very slowly in the double boiler for 1 hour, stirring occasionally. Fold in the parmesan and cayenne.

Put the bechamel into the food processor and add the cooked asparagus stalks. Activate for a few seconds before adding the egg yolks separately, giving a whizz in between. Beat the egg whites with the salt to form soft peaks.

Tip the mixture from the food processor into a bowl and carefully fold in the stiff whites. Poke the raw asparagus tips into the soufflé and scatter on a little extra parmesan. Bake in a 190°C oven for about 40 minutes or until puffed and golden.

Serve immediately.

SERVES 6

Paul Levy, Oxford, England

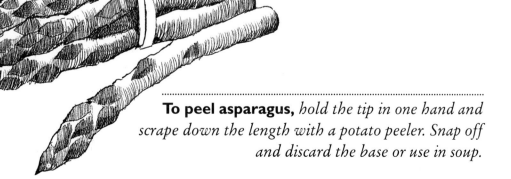

To peel asparagus, *hold the tip in one hand and scrape down the length with a potato peeler. Snap off and discard the base or use in soup.*

ASPARAGUS TARTLET WITH EGGS

Ingredients per person

puff pastry (leftovers)
individual 11 cm tart tins
4-5 spears fresh asparagus
2 eggs
pinch salt
black pepper, freshly ground
50 g butter

Roll out the pastry thinly and line the tart tins. Prick the pastry very well all over. Press aluminium foil all over the pastry and weight down with dried beans or rice. Chill for 20 minutes, then bake at 200°C until the pastry has 'set' into a firm shape (about 15 minutes). Remove the foil and continue baking until the pastry is browned (another 10-15 minutes).

Snap the root end off each asparagus spear and peel the stem with a sharp knife. Blanch the stems until tender but still with a crunch. Refresh in iced water to preserve the lovely green colour.

Prepare the eggs just before serving. Whisk the eggs lightly and pour into a saucepan. Add salt, pepper and the butter cut into small knobs. Warm gently and let the butter melt into the eggs without stirring. When melted and the eggs are beginning to set, whisk the mixture briskly and briefly, and remove from the heat. The eggs should be quite runny, so don't leave them in the pan to set hard—serve at once!

Spoon the eggs into the hot pastry cases. Re-warm the asparagus and arrange on top of the eggs.

Jenny Ferguson, New South Wales

BROAD BEANS WITH CHIVES

Serve steamed broad beans tossed in butter with chives. Or make into a salad with garlic, chives, baby yellow tomatoes, good-quality olive oil and cracked pepper.

Faye McLeish, Victoria

To refresh celery, *place it in a container, cover with water, add a washed, unpeeled potato and refrigerate for a few hours.*

CREAMED MUSHROOMS WITH POACHED EGG AND PROSCIUTTO

Ingredients per person

*1 tablespoon dried cepes or
    porcini mushrooms*
1 teaspoon butter
*1 tablespoon spring onions,
    finely sliced*
*4 medium cultivated
    mushrooms, sliced*
*1-2 oyster mushrooms
    (depending on size), sliced*
black pepper, freshly ground
1 slice prosciutto
¼ cup cream
1 large egg
*1 piece toasted white bread,
    5 cm across*
*1 tablespoon chives, finely
    chopped*

Soak the dried mushroom in cold water for at least half an hour, then strain the water through a fine kitchen cloth and reserve half a cup.

Melt the butter in a frypan. Put in the spring onions and all the mushrooms and cook briskly until softened. Season with black pepper. Remove any fat from the prosciutto, slice the meat into thin strips and stir into the mushrooms. Pour in the reserved mushroom water and boil until almost completely evaporated. Stir in the cream and boil for a minute to thicken.

Bring a saucepanful of water to a gentle simmer. Break in the egg and stir the water so the egg doesn't stick to the bottom. Cook for about 3 minutes. When the white is firm and the yolk still soft to touch, take the egg from the water with a slotted spoon, drain, and trim off the edges neatly.

To serve, pile the mushroom and prosciutto mixture in the centre of a plate. Spoon on the creamy sauce. Put the toasted round of bread on top, the poached egg on top of that, and the fine chives all over the egg. Serve at once.

Fran Gerard, South Australia

To prepare dried mushrooms *for cooking, soak them in warm water to cover for 30-60 minutes. The soaking water is often useful for soup or stock. It should, however, be well strained as many dried mushrooms contain sand.*

A REMINISCENCE OF HARICOTS BLANCS CAP AU PINET

SOME TIME in the '70s I was taken to a restaurant on one of the beaches of St Tropez. The cook was an ancient provincial lady, mother of the proprietor of L'Escole, a restaurant on the port, which was too expensive for us to go to more than once a season. The cooking was domestic and magical. The most memorable dish that evening was fresh, white haricot (or borlotti) beans, stewed gently with a point of garlic and dried cepes, probably in olive oil, and finished with crème fraîche and parsley. At least once a year I have tried to recreate this dish, but I have never really succeeded. Still, all my failures have been delicious—just not as good as that wonderful old lady's.

Paul Levy, Oxford, England

PITHIVIER OF GOAT'S CHEESE WITH BLACK OLIVE PASTE

¹/₂ kg puff pastry
¹/₂ kg goat's cheese (chèvre)
black pepper
egg wash (1 egg yolk mixed with a little olive oil and salt)
baby salad leaves
tomato quarters
chervil
black olive paste
1 cup fresh tomato sauce

Roll out the pastry to ¹/₂ cm thickness and cut 6 circles 10 cm in diameter and 4 circles 12 cm in diameter. Push the smaller rounds into small soufflé or pyrex bowls and spoon in equal quantities of goat's cheese. Add a few grinds of black pepper and top with the other rounds of pastry, pinching the sides to seal. Brush with egg wash and score the tops with a razor blade to allow steam to escape. Bake at 280°C for 4-5 minutes or until golden-brown.

To serve, arrange the salad leaves, tomato quarters and chervil, all tossed in vinaigrette, around serving plates. Dot with black olive paste. Turn out the goat's cheese pithiviers and drizzle on the fresh tomato sauce.

SERVES 6

Steve Szabo, Victoria

To refresh wilted vegetables, *soak them in cold water with a piece of charcoal. They revive miraculously.*

POTATO AND BACON PANCAKES WITH POACHED EGGS

1/2 cup chopped onion
1 1/2 cups coarsely grated,
  peeled baking potatoes
1 1/2 teaspoons salt
1/4 teaspoon freshly ground
  pepper
2 slices lean bacon, chopped
4 large eggs
1 cup watercress hollandaise
  (see below)
watercress sprigs for garnish

You will need four 10 cm
metal rings to keep the
eggs in shape.

In a bowl, combine the onion, potatoes, salt and pepper. Divide the bacon pieces into the four metal rings, set 5 cm apart on a non-stick griddle. Arrange half a cup of the potato mixture on top of each round, patting it out to cover the bacon completely. Cook at a moderate heat for 5-10 minutes, or until the undersides are brown. Turn and cook for 5 minutes more. Put pancakes in the oven at 300°C to finish cooking.

Poach the eggs in salted water. Remove with a slotted spoon and gently pat dry with paper towels. Arrange the pancakes on heated breakfast plates. Top each one with a poached egg and spoon over some of the hollandaise. Garnish each serving with the cress sprigs. Serve the remaining hollandaise separately.

SERVES 4

Fran Gerard, South Australia

WATERCRESS HOLLANDAISE

1 cup packed rinsed
  watercress leaves
1/2 cup unsalted butter
yolks of 2 large eggs
4 teaspoons fresh lemon
  juice
2 teaspoons Dijon-style
  mustard
1/4 teaspoon salt and white
  pepper

Blanch the watercress in boiling water until wilted. Drain and refresh in cold water. Spin dry. Melt the butter over moderate heat and keep it warm. In a blender, combine the egg yolks, lemon juice, mustard, watercress, salt and pepper. Process for 5 seconds. Scrape down the sides and repeat. With the motor running, add the butter in a thin stream. Season with salt and pepper to taste.

The hollandaise may be kept warm for up to 20 minutes in a bowl covered with a buttered round of wax paper in a pan of warm water.

MAKES ABOUT I CUP

Fran Gerard, South Australia

SAGE FRITTERS

BRENDA and Godfrey Gardiner run the Miners Cottage in Cockatoo Valley on the edge of the Barossa Valley, South Australia. Brenda provides delicious cooked breakfasts, picnic hampers and evening meals on request. She has supplied this simple recipe using ingredients from her kitchen garden. These fritters are a delicious accompaniment to warmed goat's cheese.

36 large fresh sage leaves
20 g (1 tablespoon) butter
125 ml (½ cup) water
125 g (½ cup) flour
pinch salt
65 ml (¼ cup) milk
1 extra-large egg white
vegetable oil for frying

Wash and dry the sage leaves carefully to avoid bruising. In a pan melt the butter with the water over a low heat. Cool. Mix the flour and salt in a bowl. Gradually beat in the butter/water mixture. Add the milk and beat until completely smooth. Cover and stand at room temperature for an hour before using.

Preheat the oven to 150°C. Heat about 2 cm oil in a heavy skillet until hot enough for a small drop of batter to turn brown quickly when dropped in the pan. Beat the egg white until stiff but not dry and gently fold into the batter. Dip a few sage leaves into the batter and drop them one at a time into the hot oil. Do not overcrowd the pan. Fry until golden brown, turning once during the cooking. Remove the fritters with a slotted spoon and keep warm in the oven until all fritters are cooked. Serve immediately.

Brenda Gardiner, South Australia

To prepare *a special, easy sweet potato dish, cook the potatoes, peel and slice when cool. Arrange the slices in a dish and pour over a mixture of orange juice, cream, butter, freshly grated nutmeg, salt and pepper. Bake in the oven until golden and crisp on top.*

SPICED YELLOW PUMPKIN

500 g yellow pumpkin
3 tablespoons oil
3 tablespoons toor dhal
1 teaspoon black mustard
  seeds
1 sprig fresh curry leaves
2 cloves garlic, finely
  chopped
2 teaspoons ground
  coriander
1 teaspoon ground cumin
1/2 teaspoon ground turmeric
1 teaspoon salt, or to taste
3 tablespoons fresh grated
  coconut

Peel and seed the pumpkin and cut into small cubes. In a saucepan heat the oil and on low heat fry the toor dhal, mustard seeds and curry leaves until dhal is golden and the mustard seeds pop. Add the garlic and stir for a minute, then stir in the ground spices. Put in the pumpkin and just enough water to almost cover the cubes. Add salt.

Cover the pan and simmer until pumpkin is half cooked, then sprinkle in the coconut and continue cooking until the pumpkin is tender. Serve with rice or chapatis.

SERVES 4

Charmaine Solomon, New South Wales

FRESH PASTA WITH WALNUTS

1 clove garlic
90 g (3/4 cup) fresh walnuts
250 ml (1 cup) cream
125 ml (1/2 cup) hot water
salt
60 g (3 tablespoons) soft
  butter
125 g (1 cup) freshly grated
  parmesan cheese
400 g fresh pasta

In a food processor whiz the garlic with the walnuts until finely chopped. Add the cream and blend for 10 seconds. Add the hot water and a little salt and blend again before adding the butter and cheese. Cook and drain the pasta and toss in the sauce.

SERVES 4

Lois Daish, New Zealand

While cooking baked potatoes, *combine some freshly grated cheese tossed in a little curry powder. When the potatoes are cooked, sprinkle the cheese on the cut side and put under the griller. When the cheese has melted and the mixture is golden brown, serve immediately.*

ZUCCHINI BLOSSOMS STUFFED WITH TUNA

20 large zucchini blossoms
100 g tinned Italian tuna,
    drained and mashed with
    a fork
1 egg
30 g freshly grated parmesan
30-50 g stale breadcrumbs,
    to make a firm mixture
tiny pinch salt
freshly ground pepper

Remove the pistil from each blossom. Combine all the farce ingredients and carefully put about a tablespoonful into each blossom. Cook quickly in sizzling butter and serve with a fresh tomato sauce.

TOMATO SAUCE
800 g tin peeled tomatoes
1 medium onion, chopped
1 sprig each parsley and
    rosemary
1 celery stalk, chopped
bay leaf
pinch sugar
10 ml each white wine
    vinegar and olive oil
1 chilli, chopped (optional)
50 ml tomato paste
2 stems basil

This tomato sauce freezes well and can be used with pasta, fish or vegetables.

Put all the ingredients in a pan and simmer until the tomatoes have reduced and the sauce is almost a purée. Pass through a fine sieve and season with salt and pepper.

Margie Agostini, New South Wales

Freezing seems *to enhance the flavour of sweet potatoes. Bake them in their skins, peel and wrap well, then freeze. Defrosted, whipped and enriched with melted butter, a little brandy and freshly grated nutmeg, they make a delicious covering for a casserole.*

ZUCCHINI FLOWERS

Di Dunlop writes:

I find this the very best way to eat zucchini flowers cut straight from the plant and still moistened with morning dew. It makes the perfect breakfast, for the most fastidious cannot resist the beauty and crisp delicacy of these fritters.

You will need 1 egg for every 6 flowers. Beat the eggs lightly with a fork. Fill a pan 1 cm deep with good olive oil. Put it over heat but do not allow it to get too hot. Dip each flower in the beaten egg and place in the pan. Turn immediately so that the egg does not run off. Cook for a few minutes and eat as soon as possible with a little salt and pepper.

ZUCCHINI FLOWER FRITTATA

*10 zucchini (preferably
    Lebanese)*
10 large eggs
*2 tablespoons grated
    parmesan*
1 clove garlic, crushed
salt and pepper
30-40 zucchini flowers
*approx. 250 ml (1 cup) olive
    oil*

Using a food processor grate the zucchini. Heat 2 tablespoons olive oil in a large heavy pan and toss half the zucchini in to rid them of moisture. Repeat with the rest of the zucchini.

Beat the eggs and add the cheese, garlic, salt and pepper. Stir in the warm zucchini. Add more oil to the pan and when hot pour in the mixture. Cover the surface of the frittata thickly with zucchini flowers that you have dipped first in olive oil. Place the pan in the oven at 200°C until set. Cool, then slide out onto a large platter and serve.

SERVES 8

Di Dunlop, Victoria

To make potato chip baskets, *peel and slice potatoes very finely. Dip a double wire mesh basket into hot oil, remove, then line the larger one with an overlapping layer of potato slices. Push the smaller basket into place. Plunge into hot oil and deep-fry until golden brown.*

◇ ◇ ◇ NOTES ◇ ◇ ◇

Remove the green centre *of garlic or*
shallots before slicing to avoid a bitter taste.

Seafood

.
.
.
.
.
.
.
.
.

CHILLI MUD CRAB

IN MELBOURNE in the late 70s there was a solitary Thai restaurant and not a single Vietnamese or Malaysian-Nonya restaurant. Today, one restaurant guide lists no fewer than 14 Thai, 16 Vietnamese and 34 Malay restaurants. The great Australian backyard is now sprouting lemongrass, coriander and Vietnamese mint along with the parsley, sage and basil, and a new generation of chefs, fluent in French and Italian, have become eloquent in Asian. Sydney's David Thompson, Neil Perry and Phillip Searle, Adelaide's Cheong Liew, Le Tu Thai, Kate Sparrow and Cedric Eu, Melbourne's Iain Hewitson, Stephanie Alexander and George Lee are all creating something far more important than the tastes of Thailand, Singapore and China. They are producing Australian food: an intelligent combination of bold, single-minded flavours and tantalising textures crafted from the best produce this country has to offer.

While the star of this dish is Queensland mud crab, the technique is Singaporean and the flavourings are Thai.

1 fresh live crab
1 stalk lemongrass
½ cup peanut oil
2 teaspoons fresh ginger, finely chopped
2 cloves garlic, bruised
2 fresh chillies, finely chopped
2 cm knob galangal, finely chopped
2 kaffir lime leaves
½ cup fish sauce
½ cup tomato ketchup
1 tablespoon chilli sauce
½ cup hot water
spring onions, coriander and Asian mint to garnish

Drown the crab in a pot of fresh water for an hour or two. Remove the top shell and scrape out the fibrous tissue and stomach. Take off the claws and crack lightly with a hammer or mallet, then cut the body into 6 pieces, each with the legs attached. Peel the lemongrass and finely slice the tender white stalk.

Heat the wok and add the oil. When the oil is very hot, fry the crab pieces until they change colour, turning them to cook through. Remove the crab and keep in a warm place.

Turn the heat to low and fry the ginger, garlic, chillies, galangal, lime leaves and lemongrass for 4-5 minutes. When cooked but not browned add the fish sauce, ketchup, chilli sauce and hot water. Bring to the boil, stirring. Then return the crab to the sauce and simmer for 3 minutes until the crab is fully cooked. Adjust sauces if necessary.

Garnish with spring onions, coriander and fresh Asian mint and serve with steamed jasmine rice.

SERVES 2

Terry Durack, Victoria

CRAYFISH, CORIANDER AND GINGER SANDWICHES FOR PICNICS

2 small cooked crayfish
1 small cucumber
1 x 1 cm piece fresh ginger
6 stalks coriander
10 tablespoons mayonnaise
salt and pepper
1 loaf brown whole-grain
    bread
butter
cress to garnish

MAYONNAISE
2 egg yolks
1 teaspoon French mustard
salt and pepper
2 cups peanut oil
white vinegar

Remove the crayfish meat from the shells and claws. Cut it into small pieces. Peel the cucumber, remove the watery seeds and cut the flesh into very fine julienne. Peel and slice the ginger very finely. Tear the coriander leaves into small pieces.

Combine crayfish, coriander, ginger, cucumber and just enough mayonnaise to moisten in a bowl, folding carefully. Add salt and pepper to taste.

Butter the bread with soft butter. Onto each slice spoon 1-2 tablespoons of crayfish mixture and fold the slice over. Tap to spread mixture evenly and then remove crusts. Slice into 2 wedges, place in a box and garnish with cress.

Mayonnaise: Put the yolks in a bowl with the mustard, salt and pepper. Slowly whisk in the oil, beating constantly until all the oil has been incorporated. Thin down with a little vinegar to the desired thickness.

MAKES ABOUT 20 SANDWICHES

Anita Hughes, Victoria

OCEAN TROUT, RAW WITH CHILLI DRESSING

410 g fresh ocean trout fillet,
    in one piece
4 small chillies, chopped
    finely
3 tablespoons chopped
    parsley
20 ml (4 teaspoons) olive oil
juice of a lemon, strained
freshly ground pepper

Slice the fillet as finely as possible. Scatter on the chillies and parsley. Drizzle on the olive oil. Immediately before serving, pour on the lemon juice and add the pepper.

SERVES 4

Tony Sassi, Far North Queensland

MAH MEE, OR CHINESE NOODLES

DURING 1973 we lived in Singapore. East-meets-West flavours had barely touched the menus in Australia and I knew little about Asian cooking. After we had settled in, I determined to take advantage of every opportunity I could to make the year a real learning experience.

I set off daily to the markets—the big one in Orchard Road, run by Cold Storage, was a fascinating new world. Fruit and vegetables I had never seen before were there in abundance and I felt like a child in a sweet shop. I would buy systematically and return home to the lovely Malaysian girl who had moved in to cook for us. Salmah taught in her own simple way how to prepare what I had purchased. It was the first time I had seen quail's eggs, and I delighted in using these in salads and noodle dishes. Exotic fruits were inexpensive and delicious and there were pungent herbs like coriander that I had never tasted before. Chillies were a new sensation and I marvelled that something so tiny could be so potent.

Overwhelmed by so many riches, I signed up for classes to explore them more fully. Through them I began to unravel some of the mysteries of Asian cooking. My teacher, Mrs Benjamin, lived a long way from me and the journey had to be undertaken by bus. That was an experience in itself, as twenty years ago Singapore was not as organised as it is today. There was no hot water in Mrs Benjamin's kitchen and the ironing was piled high in the corner of the room. It always made me feel guilty, as Salmah was taking care of my huge pile at home.

I learnt a lot in that tiny kitchen. We started from scratch every day. First you had to grind your spices and pulverise your almonds on large granite slabs. I loved every minute of it and, as the mysteries unfolded, I began to understand how impossible the task was and how much there was for a Westerner to learn.

Most people we knew had cooks, and they became another source of learning for me. A favourite pastime was to sit in the kitchen and watch these women prepare from scratch what were, to me, complicated meals. Many didn't speak English, so I simply observed and wrote as I sat. Bats were caught and cooked for medicinal purposes. Snake and offal from various animals were included and often disguised in noodle dishes and soups—for instance, pig's intestine was chopped and added to the breakfast porridge, and pig's appendix was floated in soups. I watched the chopping, pounding and pulverising, fascinated at the time and energy it took to prepare a meal from scratch, completely by hand.

Sitting on a small stool close to the floor, I watched the Chinese cook of our next-door neighbour prepare our favourite noodles. I wrote down exactly what she did and produce the noodles the same way every now and then on request. I have never tasted better mah mee—we serve it on a huge platter and my children used to eat every skerrick. It takes time, but then Eastern cooks never work at the frenetic pace we tend to.

▶

1 kg raw unpeeled prawns
2 teaspoons sugar
good pinch salt
750 g pork fillet
8 stalks choy sum, preferably
  with yellow flowers
1 bunch coriander
1 bunch spring onions
250 g bean shoots, trimmed
  of root end
3 red chillies
3 garlic cloves
4 shallots
2 teaspoons soy sauce
2 teaspoons cornflour
1/2 cup plus 1 tablespoon
  peanut oil
450 g or 2 packets Chinese
  egg noodles

PORK MARINADE
1 teaspoon cornflour
1 teaspoon sugar
1 teaspoon salt
1/4 teaspoon white pepper
1 tablespoon dark soy sauce

Peel and de-vein the prawns. Place in a basin with the sugar and salt. Put the shells in a pot, cover with water and simmer for 10 minutes. Reserve the stock. Slice the pork finely and marinate for one hour in the prepared mixture.

Cut the choy sum stalks diagonally into 5 cm lengths. Wash the coriander and tear into small pieces. Slice the chillies lengthways and remove the seeds. Chop finely (if you like it hot, slice the chillies into small rounds leaving the seeds in). Finely chop the garlic and shallots.

Bring the prawn water to the boil and cook the noodles in it for 5 minutes. Strain, reserving 2¹/₂ cups of the liquid. Cool and add soy sauce and cornflour to the liquid and set aside.

Put ¹/₂ cup peanut oil into a large wok. When hot, fry the strained noodles for a few minutes, tossing constantly. Remove to a warm platter and keep hot. Add the extra tablespoons of oil to the wok and fry the garlic and shallots. Add the marinated pork and the prawns. Cook through then add the remaining vegetables. Pour on the cooled prawn stock. When the vegetables are cooked but still crisp, spoon the mixture onto the noodles and garnish with fresh coriander.

SERVES 8

Penny Smith, Victoria

To remove fish odour *from a pan,*
empty used tea leaves into it, fill with
water and leave standing for 10 minutes.

MUSSELS WITH EGGS

*48 mussels, cleaned
    thoroughly*
2 shallots, finely sliced
50 ml water
1 cup dry white wine
unsalted butter
a little oil
*3 tablespoons each carrots,
    onions and celery, diced*
salt and pepper
8 eggs
*8 slices bread cut into scone
    shapes and deep fried*

SAUCE
2 tablespoons unsalted butter
2¹/₂ heaped tablespoons flour
pinch saffron
*2 yolk portion hollandaise
    sauce*

HOLLANDAISE SAUCE
*3 tablespoons white wine
    vinegar*
6 pepper corns
¹/₂ bayleaf
2 blades mace
2 egg yolks
*125 g butter cut into small
    cubes*
salt

Place the mussels in a heavy pot with the shallots, water and wine. Shake the pot over heat until the mussels open. Remove them from the shell and keep warm in a clean saucepan with 2 tablespoons of the cooking liquid.

Melt the oil and butter in a pan, add the diced vegetables and sauté gently until tender. Season with salt and pepper.

Strain the mussel cooking liquid through two layers of muslin. Pour into a saucepan. Heat to simmer and poach the eggs for 3-3¹/₂ minutes. Drain and place the eggs on the croûtons. Strain the liquid and reserve.

Sauce: Melt the butter, add the flour and whisk in the mussel liquid until mixture has thickened. Add the vegetable mixture and bring to the boil. Cook for a few minutes, then pour through a conical sieve into a saucepan. Add a good pinch of saffron.

Using a whisk, blend a little prepared hollandaise into the mussel sauce. Coat the eggs with the sauce, and serve.

Hollandaise Sauce: Put the vinegar, peppercorns, bayleaf and mace into a small, thick saucepan and reduce to a tablespoon. Cream the yolks in a bowl with a nut-sized piece of softened butter and a good pinch of salt. Strain the hot vinegar onto the yolks. Mix thoroughly and return to the saucepan. Over a very gentle heat continue to whisk adding butter constantly until the sauce is shiny and thick and all the butter has been incorporated.

SERVES 4

Paul Grischy, Far North Queensland

....

Fresh fish *is best stored in the refrigerator on a plate covered with foil. It is inedible after 6 days.*

SALMON GRILLED WITH A HERB AND TOMATO CRUST

5 medium tomatoes
1/2 small brown onion
1 stalk celery
1 medium carrot
1 clove garlic
black pepper, freshly ground
400 g broad beans
40 ml (2 tablespoons) olive
    oil
1 teaspoon chopped
    tarragon
1 tablespoon chopped
    parsley
1 teaspoon chopped basil
4 slices salmon fillet, about
    120 g each

Cut tomatoes, onion, celery and carrot into small pieces and place in a saucepan with the garlic and a little pepper. Cook on medium heat for about 30 minutes. Pass this sauce through a mouli or fine strainer and return it to the pan.

Shell broad beans and place in boiling water for 1 minute. Drain beans and, using a small knife, carefully remove the outer skin. Add peeled broad beans to tomato sauce.

Brush salmon fillets with olive oil and cook on a grill or barbecue for 2-3 minutes on each side, depending on their thickness.

Gently stir the herbs and remaining olive oil into reheated tomato sauce. Spoon sauce onto plates before carefully arranging salmon fillets on top.

SERVES 4

Gabriel Gaté, Victoria

When presented *with several fish you cannot cook at once, paint them quickly with a thin layer of light soy sauce and put them trustingly into the refrigerator. Cook them up to 3 days later and they will taste newly caught and have absolutely no hint of soy. Excellent for chops and steak too.*

SALMON IN BASIL BUTTER

COOK THIS recipe in summer and use only fresh basil and fresh, ripe tomatoes.

4 small ripe tomatoes
40 g butter
salt
150 g unsalted butter
20 basil leaves, coarsely
    chopped
juice of 1 lemon
salt and freshly ground
    pepper
1 shallot
1 piece celery
1 piece leek
1 litre water
100 ml dry white wine
5 peppercorns
110 g rock salt
8 slices salmon, 80 g each,
    cut off boned fillet

Peel, seed and chop the tomatoes into fine dice. Melt 40 g butter in a pan and sweat the tomato. Season with salt and set aside.

Prepare the basil butter by putting the unsalted butter, chopped basil leaves, lemon juice, pepper and salt into a small bowl. Set the bowl over a pan of cold water. Bring the water to the boil, stirring the butter mixture constantly. When the mixture has thickened, strain and set aside.

Chop the shallot, celery and leek. Bring a litre of water to the boil with the wine and chopped vegetables, peppercorns and salt. Add the salmon medallions and turn off the heat. Poach the fish in this liquid for 3-4 minutes, depending on the thickness of the fillet.

To serve, pour even pools of basil sauce onto preheated dinner plates. Place 2 poached salmon fillets in the centre of each plate and garnish with the stewed tomatoes. Serve immediately.

SERVES 4

Klaus Lemm, Victoria

'**Mr Joseph Sinel,** *who made experiments on behalf of the RSPCA, came to the conclusion that a lobster put into cold water which is slowly brought to the boil, collapses and dies painlessly when the heat reaches 70 degrees.'*
Elizabeth David

SALMON MOUSSE, SMOKED, WITH YARRA VALLEY CHÈVRE

WALTER BOURKE is a cheesemaker and restaurateur. He offers delicious fare in his restaurant and when he is not cooking for his customers he is making cheese with enthusiasm and expertise. His tiny rounds of goat's cheese are covered with charcoal ash and sit beautifully on croûtons drizzled with virgin olive oil and popped under a hot grill. A little piece of sun-dried tomato, a few tiny thyme leaves, or even a jewel of roasted, peeled red pepper add to this cheese's unctuousness. Walter's cheeses can be purchased at several of Melbourne's leading delicatessens.

250 g Yarra Valley chèvre
25 g smoked salmon
1 tablespoon finely chopped
  onion
10 g sun-dried tomatoes in
  oil, roughly chopped
2 tablespoons oil from the
  tomato jar
freshly ground white pepper
fresh bread slices or croûtons

Mix crumbled chèvre, roughly chopped salmon, onion, tomatoes, oil and pepper together carefully. Spread onto bread or croûtons and warm slightly in the oven before serving.

Walter Bourke, Victoria

YABBIES ON BRIOCHE

Prepare your favourite brioche recipe (or see page 115)—without sugar, but with a generous pinch of saffron threads. Mould and bake in a brioche loaf tin.

Slice the brioche 2 cm thick, lightly brush with the best olive oil and toast in a warm oven until golden. Allow 6 yabbies per serve, boiled in a court-bouillon until just turned pink, and cooled and peeled.

On top of the brioche slices, layer a pleasing combination of the following: oiled and grilled slices of eggplant; red and yellow peppers grilled and peeled; artichoke hearts preserved in olive oil; sliced dried tomatoes; slices of sun-ripened tomatoes; golden or baby red beetroot, boiled until tender, sliced and tossed in walnut oil; French beans, blanched al dente, immediately tossed in olive oil and pepper; fine slices of patrone potatoes.

Stack the yabbies on top of your arrangement and serve with a mayonnaise flavoured with a purée of basil and pinenuts or perfumed with a purée of roasted garlic.

Marieke Brugman, Victoria

To prepare a good crumb mixture, *combine a well-beaten egg with 1 teaspoon of oil, 1 dessertspoon of milk, a pinch of salt and a few chopped herbs. Dip the ingredients intended for frying into the mixture and then cover with breadcrumbs.*

Poultry

CHICKEN CHOP SUEY

ELIZABETH CHONG writes:

One morning my postman asked me where he could go to get some 'real Chinese like the way it was in the good old days'. He was of course referring to the style of Chinese food that evolved during the days of the goldfields, and which was exemplified in the little cafes which sprang up.

The Chung Weh Cafe, a 'high-class Chinese restaurant' in Heffernan Lane, Melbourne, opened its doors in 1921, operated until 1989, and was a byword for every devotee of Chinese food. The menu listed 15 different types of chop suey, ranging from pork and chicken to lobster and pineapple. Everyone knew what they were getting and it would not have occurred to them that the dish was unknown in China!

How was chop suey born? One evening (the story goes), some hungry diggers returned late from the goldfields and demanded that their Chinese cooks prepare a meal for them. As the little eating house had closed for the night and there was very little food on the premises, the cooks had to call on their imagination to produce enough food for their customers. They found a little bit of this and a little bit of that, and tossed them together in a sizzling wok with a dash of sauce and seasoning.

The European diggers were astonished with what they saw and tasted and wanted to known the name of the dish. The Chinese cooks shrugged nonchalantly: 'Oh, chop suey...' (or, more correctly, 'darp sui', which means 'a little bit of this and a little bit of that').

Here is my version of how I think the original 'chicken chop suey' was cooked.

cooking oil
few slices fresh ginger
small handful chicken meat from breast or leg, cut into bite-size pieces
selected vegetables (Chinese cabbage, broccoli, celery, capsicum, zucchini, onion), sliced into 5 cm lengths
a little salt and sugar
1/3 cup water
dash light soy sauce
1/2 teaspoon cornflour mixed with 2 tablespoons water

Heat the wok for a minute or two, add a little cooking oil and heat until just beginning to smoke. Add the ginger slices to sizzle a little and then stir-fry the chicken pieces until they change colour (about 1 or 2 minutes). Remove to a plate and wipe out the wok with some kitchen paper.

Heat a little more oil in the wok, add salt and then toss all the vegetables together over high heat until glazed. Add a little sugar and 1/3 cup water. Cover the wok with a lid and cook the vegetables over high heat for a further 2 minutes before returning the chicken to the wok.

Combine the chicken and vegetables quickly, sprinkle in the soy sauce, and stir the cornflour thickening into the centre of the wok until the sauce is light and velvety. Serve with steamed rice or noodles.

SERVES 4

Elizabeth Chong, Victoria

CHICKEN FLAVOURED WITH ANCHOVY

1 x no. 10 chicken

MARINADE
a little oil
1 teaspoon anchovy purée
50 ml lemon juice
50 ml vegetable oil
1 teaspoon Dijon mustard
fresh rosemary, chervil,
    tarragon and parsley,
    chopped

SAUCE
50 ml madeira
200 ml rich brown stock
100 ml cream
1 tablespoon chives, freshly
    snipped

Combine all the marinade ingredients. Coat the chicken thoroughly and leave to stand for at least 12 hours.

Pat the chicken dry and pan-fry in a little oil over a high heat to brown. Turn the heat down and cook gently to crisp the skin. To finish cooking, put the chicken in a 200°C oven for 10 minutes. Set aside and keep warm.

Sauce: Deglaze the pan with madeira, pour in the stock and reduce by half. Add the cream and reduce again until the sauce is thickened. Toss in the chives before serving.

To serve, cut the chicken into 4 pieces, coat each with the hot sauce and serve with a crispy cos lettuce salad.

SERVES 2

Robert Licciardo, Victoria

Trim chicken livers *before using, being careful to remove the tiny green sac sometimes found in the centre. It gives a very bitter flavour and can spoil your dish completely.*

DUCK LIVER MOUSSE WITH RED WINE JELLY

MOUSSE
160 g duck livers
85 g smoked speck (pork belly fat)
1 tablespoon sultanas, soaked in 2 tablespoons brandy
1 pigeon breast, skinned and cut into small dice
2 eggs
125 ml cream
salt and pepper to taste

JELLY
1 litre red wine
150 g cooked beetroot
salt and pepper
4 sheets gelatine
2 egg whites to clarify the jelly

Mousse: Place the speck in food processor and blend for 3 minutes. Add duck livers and blend again until smooth. Add eggs, seasoning and brandy from the soaked sultanas. Blend again. Strain this mixture through a fine sieve. Mix in the cream, sultanas and pigeon breast. Pour into 4-6 (depending on the size) ramekins. Cover with foil and cook in a bain-marie in the oven at 175°C until set. Allow to cool, then refrigerate overnight.

Jelly: Bring wine to the boil, add beetroot, season and simmer for 5 minutes. Clarify with egg whites by cooling the liquid and stirring in 2 egg whites and their shells. Bring the liquid gently to the boil and when all the residue has clung to the egg white, strain the liquid through fine muslin. Soak gelatine in cold water until soft and squeeze out excess water. Reheat a small amount of red wine liquid and stir in the softened gelatine until dissolved. Add this to the rest of the wine liquid and mix well. Allow to cool.

When mousse is cold, pour over the red wine jelly and refrigerate until set. Serve with toasted brioche.

SERVES 4-6

Tansy Goode, Victoria

When using leaf gelatine, *reseal to protect the unused sheets as they lose their setting quality if left exposed to air for too long.*

FARM HOUSE TERRINE

250 g duck or chicken liver
250 g pork liver
250 g minced raw ham
500 g streaky bacon
1 onion, chopped
60 g butter
$^1\!/_2$ teaspoon dried herbs
1 sherry glass of brandy
1 wine glass of red wine
12 button mushrooms,
    chopped
300 ml cream
1 egg
black pepper

Trim and chop the livers roughly, removing any fibrous bits. Combine the livers with the ham. Line the terrine with bacon strips, leaving enough length to overlap and cover the top. Sauté the onion in butter and add the herbs and brandy. Set alight and when the flame subsides, pour in the red wine. Add the mushrooms and stir for a few minutes before removing from the heat and adding the cream and egg. Season with black pepper and salt to taste.

Heat the oven to 175°C. Put the pâté mixture into the prepared terrine and cover with the bacon flaps and foil. Place in a bain-marie and bake at 175°C for 1½ hours. Cool before refrigerating with a heavy weight on top. When fully chilled, serve turned out onto a platter or straight from the terrine.

SERVES 6-8

Wendy Robinson, Victoria

Chicken and duck skins *make delicious linings for terrines and are not nearly as fatty as the traditional pork fat or speck.*

POLLO RIPIENA RINASCENTE

1 x 1.7 kg chicken
1-5 eggs
butter
lots of parsley
salt and pepper
8-10 ham slices off the bone
oil and butter for roasting

SAUCE
300 ml strong chicken stock
250 g chopped mushrooms

Cut the chicken open down the back and bone it out so that it can be laid fully open. Leave the wing and leg bones in place. Prepare the omelette: whisk the eggs, season and add lots of chopped parsley. Cook until firm and lay on a plate to cool.

Arrange some of the slices of ham to cover the inside of the chicken and place the omelette on top. Cover this with more slices of ham. Re-form the chicken to shape, pleating the skin folds to hold. (You shouldn't need to sew.) Put the chicken in a baking dish, right side up, season with salt and pepper and pour on a little oil. Roast in the oven at 220°C for 45 minutes, until cooked. Allow to cool before slicing.

Sauce: Pour off some of the grease from the roasting pan, deglaze with the stock and add the mushrooms. Reduce and season.

This dish is wonderful served cold for picnics.

SERVES 4

Wendy Robinson, Victoria

When cooking a sauce *that contains olive oil, add a little uncooked oil at the end to freshen the taste of the dish.*

QUAIL WITH LIVER MOUSSE SERVED WITH A PORT WINE JELLY

MOUSSE
*400 g chicken livers,
    trimmed
50 ml port
salt and pepper
200 ml cream*

*6 quail, boned (split down
    the back, leaving the
    breast and skin intact)
600 g liver mousse
1 litre good stock made from
    quail bones and extra
    chicken seasoning and no
    fat*

JELLY
*1 litre quail stock
200 ml port
50 ml sherry vinegar
leaf gelatine as required
    (6 sheets per 500 ml
    liquid)*

Mousse: A day in advance, purée the livers with the port and seasonings in a vitamiser. Force the mixture through a sieve into a clean bowl and stir in the cream. Butter a small terrine and pour in the mousse. Bake at 160°C in a bain-marie for 1 hour.

Fill the quails with 100 g liver mousse each. Sew up or skewer each bird securely (this is important). Heat the stock to simmer and gently poach the quails for approximately 20 minutes. Do not boil. Remove the birds and allow to cool.

Jelly: Reduce the stock, port and vinegar until the mixture measures approximately 500 ml. Soak the gelatine leaves in cold water, squeeze and stir into the warm liquid. Keep stirring until completely dissolved. Cool.

Slice the quail onto a plate. Using a brush, coat the quails with the liquid several times until it glazes. Pour the rest of the jelly onto a tin plate and refrigerate. Cut into small cubes and serve with the quail. Garnish with selected fresh vegetables.

SERVES 6

Tansy Goode, Victoria

1 sachet gelatine *equals 10 g or 3 teaspoons or 6 leaves. This amount will set 500 ml/16 fl oz of liquid to a light jelly. 30 g of powdered gelatine is equivalent to 30 g unsoaked gelatine leaves.*

STEWED DUCK WITH PARSNIP

MICHAEL HILL SMITH writes:

I find duck one of the most difficult birds to cook. Some live like battery hens and are soft, tender and flavourless, whilst others have had a hard, athletic life and have a texture like boiled rubber. Because it is often impossible to obtain the biography of every duck you buy, I avoid roasting these fickle birds and ensure they are tender when served by long, slow stewing.

2 ducks (remove oil glands
  from base of the tail)
knob of butter
5 rashers bacon
3 large brown onions
4 carrots
1 stick celery
6 small parsnips, peeled and
  grated
salt and pepper

Heat butter in a heavy pan and brown the ducks. Set ducks aside. Roughly chop the bacon, onions, carrots and celery and brown lightly in the same pan. Place all ingredients in a large stockpot or boiler. Cover with water and simmer gently until the ducks are tender (1-1½ hours).

Take the ducks from the stockpot, remove all meat from the bones and set aside. Return the bones to the stock and reduce to about 3-4 cups after straining. Chop duck pieces into large but edible size, place in a pot and cover with concentrated duck stock. Thicken with grated parsnip, season and cook for a further 15 minutes.

Serve on a bed of brown rice or half wild, half brown rice.

SERVES 4

Michael Hill Smith, South Australia

For burnt saucepans, *put 1 teaspoon of cream of tartar in water in the pan and boil for 15 minutes. Allow to stand overnight and all the burn should easily be removed.*

THAI PEPPERED CHICKEN

POTTINGERS is a very special country restaurant 1 1/2 hours' drive from Brisbane, serving Queensland seafood at its best. Other specialities include vegetables and herbs from the garden. The menu has an Eastern influence, as in this recipe.

18 chicken thigh pieces

MARINADE
180 ml vegetable oil
125 ml dark soy sauce
1/2 tablespoon black peppercorns
10 cloves garlic, peeled
1 tablespoon fresh coriander, chopped

Put all the marinade ingredients into the blender and process thoroughly. Put the chicken pieces into a stainless steel bowl, pour on the marinade and work into the chicken with your hands. Cover and leave refrigerated for at least 3 hours.

To cook, place the chicken on a rack at 200°C for 20 minutes in a convection oven or 30 minutes in an ordinary oven to crisp the skin.

Serve on wild rice and garnish with extra fresh coriander, snow peas and sweet corn or yellow squash.

SERVES 6

Lew and Penny Pottinger, Queensland

Green, black and white peppercorns *are all the same berry. Green peppercorns are unripe, black peppercorns are ripe, and white peppercorns are black ones with the outer skins removed. Pink peppercorns are the dried berries of a plant related to poison ivy.*

TURKEY BREAST WITH PISTACHIO NUTS AND ORANGE

2 chicken livers
1 tablespoon brandy
1 boned turkey fillet
250 g minced raw chicken
1 small veal escalope,
    minced
2 spring onions
1 tablespoon roasted
    pistachio nuts
2 teaspoons soy sauce
zest and juice of 1 orange
60 g unsalted butter
2 cups chicken stock
salt and freshly ground
black pepper
1/2 cup cream

Trim the chicken livers. Marinate in brandy overnight.

Holding the turkey fillet flat in the palm of your hand, make an incision almost right through and open it out like a book. Put the fillet between plastic wrap and flatten to an even thickness.

Chop the spring onion finely. Put into a basin with the minced meats, nuts, soy and orange zest. Chop the liver into small dice and add with its marinade to the chicken mixture. Season with salt and pepper and mix thoroughly.

Spread this mixture onto the bottom half of the fillet and fold the top over it. Secure with beef olive pins or sew up.

Melt the butter in a frying-pan. Gently brown the stuffed fillet on each side. Remove to a rack in a baking dish, cover with foil and bake at 180°C for half an hour.

Put the chicken stock into the frying-pan and reduce to a glaze. Add the cream and reduce until thick. Whisk in the strained orange juice, season and serve.

To serve, cut the fillet into diagonal strips, fan them onto a plate and drizzle the sauce across the top. Garnish with watercress.

SERVES 4-6

Penny Smith, Victoria

When cooking *the Christmas turkey or roasting any bird, wrap it tightly with hospital gauze. Baste the surface and it will stay moist and succulent.*

To prepare chestnuts *for cooking, score the shell and bring to the boil. Cook for a few minutes and peel while still hot. Alternatively, score and place in a hot oven (210°C) until the skins pop and then peel. To prepare purée, simmer the shelled nuts in boiling water until soft.*

Keep all nuts *in sealed containers in the freezer to retain maximum freshness. Roast in the oven to crisp them before using.*

Meats

THE CHINESE IN VICTORIA

LIFE in nineteenth-century China, especially in the southern and eastern provinces, was difficult. Civil wars, natural disasters, over-population and a stagnant economy drove millions out of the country desperately seeking some means of survival. At the same time Australia was at a stage of great development, with abundant land, and the demand for labour was strong.

The first Chinese group to arrive in Victoria came within fifteen years of the first European settlement. The date was 8 December 1848, and the reception was hardly encouraging. The local press labelled the first Chinese sojourners 'wild beasts' and 'barbarians'.

They were actually hired to come as bush workers, domestic and farm workers, and shepherds. However it was really the discovery of gold in 1851 which attracted Chinese immigration to Victoria on a large scale. Those who had come to mine gold saw themselves as sojourners, not settlers. The money they would earn on the goldfields would be sent to the families they had left behind in China.

Ships sailed to Australia from Hong Kong with their cargo of men in search of the 'New Gold Mountain'. Chinese immigrants carried their few possessions on their backs, cooking utensils among them, and vegetable seeds in their pockets. Ever mindful of the need for survival, they set about cultivating and growing their own foodstuffs in order to maintain their normal diet of rice and vegetables in this foreign land.

I have heard stories of how the European diggers were enticed by the wonderfully strange smells wafting from the Chinese camps, and how they were astonished at the sight of a Chinese cook bowing low over a sizzling wok of marvellous vegetables. Surely this could not be the food of 'wild beasts' and 'barbarians'? Soon the Europeans were requesting Chinese cooks in their camps. I strongly suspect that those diggers were the first non-Chinese in Australia to eat food prepared and cooked by Chinese cooks.

In the mid-nineteenth century there were between ten and fifteen lodging houses in Little Bourke Street, Melbourne, run by Chinese, providing accommodation for fellow countrymen on their way to the goldfields. The burgeoning community in Little Bourke Street provided for all the needs of the diggers—food, equipment and medicine.

As gold petered out and the men began to filter back to the city, new occupations had to be sought. These men were unskilled except for farming and labouring work; some turned to market gardening, some became small shopkeepers, some became fishermen in St Kilda. Others engaged in furniture-making, or growing bananas; still others opened boarding houses and cafes.

Originally these cafes were opened to cater for other Chinese, but more and more Europeans, cultivating a taste for the delectable and enticing food, began to patronise them. And so the Chinese restaurant industry was born in Australia. Its beginnings were humble; indeed, the fact that it survived at all against the odds testifies to the strength of the cuisine. Despite sharp fluctuations in their total numbers in different periods of Victoria's history, the Chinese have been

here as long as any other ethnic group. It is nothing short of a miracle that they have managed to survive discriminatory laws, immigration restrictions and something called 'Chinese protectorates', which segregated them from the main population. The frequent outbreaks of violence and occasional riots have all been amply documented.

What we do not seem to know enough about is how the Chinese withstood the hostilities of the physical and sociopolitical environments; how they persisted in using peaceful means to seek out opportunities; how they repeatedly demonstrated their loyalties to become fully-fledged citizens; and how they excelled themselves to contribute to the welfare of Australia.

The White Australia policy introduced in 1901, as well as the anti-Chinese labour laws, had a drastic effect. The only Chinese establishments which increased their numbers at this time were the cafes and restaurants, which had begun to gain in popularity during the 1920s. Many will remember with affection and nostalgia the Chung Wah cafe in Heffernan Lane, the Hong Kong cafe and the Kun Ming cafe—the latter still operating successfully in much the same manner as of old.

The period from 1947 to the early 1970s saw the continued expansion of Chinese settlement as the restrictive immigration laws were eased. It was during this period that Chinese began to settle in urban Melbourne, extending the Chinese community beyond the central business district. Chinese restaurants were established everywhere, from Toorak to Moonee Ponds. Chinese food was not only accepted, it was booming in popularity. Sunday night in the suburbs was 'Chinese takeaway' night. Housewives would queue to fill their pots and billies with chicken and almonds and fried rice to take home to the family. The food was healthy, delicious and cheap.

In the 1960s the cuisine began to take on new dimensions. A better-travelled and gradually more discerning public was becoming aware that there was much more to Chinese food than just chop suey and dim sims. Restaurants like the Golden Phoenix, Oriental Gourmet, Empress of China, and Flower Drum showed a totally new face to lovers of Chinese food. Master chefs flown in from Hong Kong introduced Melburnians to a new, delicate Chinese cuisine, served in elegant surroundings. They led the field in establishing the standard of food served in Melbourne's Chinatown today.

Today the cabinet-makers and lodging houses of Little Bourke Street have gone to make way for top-class restaurants. Of all the customs and traditions the early settlers brought with them to Australia, the food and its philosophy have flourished, remained and become firmly entrenched in the social fabric and lifestyle of Australia. The history of Australian-Chinese interactions is a part of Australian heritage. The telling of this fascinating story can only promote greater intercultural understanding, and the history of Chinese food in Australia is a compelling part of that story.

Perhaps China's food is her greatest missionary, and perhaps world peace may yet be achieved—not around the conference table, but around the dining tables of the world.

Elizabeth Chong, Victoria

BEEF AND TOMATOES

BEEF AND Tomatoes was also a popular dish in Chinese restaurants up to the 1950s, when it seemed to die a somewhat natural death.

I remember this was a favourite dish of my grandmother's and appeared on our family table long after she passed away; we still cook and enjoy this home-style dish regularly, and I am surprised when friends ask me if it is truly 'Chinese'. My belief is that anything, if fresh, can be cooked 'in Chinese'. Those early Chinese diggers simply utilised whatever was at hand, and with Chinese ingenuity, worked their own magic. Thus Beef and Tomatoes 'Australian style' was born.

6 medium ripe tomatoes,
   quartered
1 white onion, chopped
315 g minced beef (rump)
2 cloves garlic
3 tablespoons cooking oil
2 teaspoons sugar
$^1/_2$ teaspoon salt
$^1/_2$ teaspoon pepper
2 stalks spring onions, cut
   into 4 cm lengths

Heat the oil in the wok, add the salt and garlic and sizzle gently (don't burn the garlic). Add the onions, fry lightly for a minute and then add the minced beef. Toss quickly over high heat until the meat changes colour, add the tomatoes and toss well.

Add the sugar and pepper, cover with lid and simmer for 6-7 minutes. Toss through the spring onions and serve with steamed rice.

Elizabeth Chong, Victoria

Green papaya *pieces or ripe papaya is used in the East as a tenderiser. Add cubes of green papaya to your meat casserole or smear papaya purée onto cheaper cuts and allow to stand before cooking.*

BETHANY CORNED SILVERSIDE

UNA GRAY writes:

I have always wanted to cook. I was the youngest of a family of eight children and I suppose there was always cooking taking place but my real inspiration came during the World War II years, when my parents decided that I, at age 11, should be evacuated out of Melbourne to a guest house in Healesville called Bethany. I spent two years there with Millie and Sam Cameron, who had no children of their own.

Millie had trained as a pastry-cook somewhere in the Riverina District and was a wonderful all-round cook, but she really excelled with sponge cakes, pastries, brandy snaps and butterfly cakes. I was allowed to wrap the brandy snaps around greased wooden spoons very quickly as soon as they came out of the oven.

The oven was part of an enormous black stove (which Sam used to polish with stove-black once a week until it glistened) with a large water fountain down one side and a shining brass tap at the bottom. There was no such thing as a hot water service, so Sam would keep the water fountain full—it provided all the water for washing dishes and for the shaving mugs. The bathrooms had only chip bath-heaters, so male guests, towels over their shoulders, would come into the kitchen to shave and would always stop for a chat.

2-3 kg piece corned silverside
1 large onion
½ cup vinegar
½ teaspoon each black peppercorns, yellow mustard seeds, fenugreek
1 star anise
6 cloves
2 cloves garlic
2 thick slices green ginger
1 tablespoon raw sugar
1 carrot
1 parsnip (optional)

MUSTARD SAUCE
1 egg
1 tablespoon English mustard
3 dessertspoons sugar
1 cup of stock from the beef and vegetables
scant cup white vinegar

Rinse the meat in cold water. Place in a pot, cover with cold water and bring to a gentle boil. Discard the water, rinse the meat and the pot and then return the meat to the pot with all the other ingredients. Add water to cover the meat, bring to the boil and simmer gently for approximately 1 hour per kilo of meat.

Mustard Sauce: Whisk the egg in a small saucepan. Moisten the mustard with a little beef juice and add it to the egg with the sugar. Then add the rest of the beef liquid and vinegar. Stir constantly over a gentle heat until the mixture thickens. Do not boil or re-heat as it may curdle.

Serve hot with parsley, mixed herbs or mustard sauce. Any meat left over should be returned to the cooking liquid to cool. It will be delicious served cold with salad or in sandwiches.

Una Gray, Queensland

COUNTRY CURED HAM

'BURRABILLA Jilla, champion Large White sow, is a very exotic pig,' says her owner and breeder Sandy Radbone of Burrabirra, Ngapala. A veteran of the agricultural show ring, they know her from Emu Downs to Black Springs and Brady Creek. Ms Radbone, who won her first big pig prize at the Eudunda show ten years ago, has a soft spot for Large Whites, though she says they are the very devil to breed.

What makes a good pig? 'A lovely long straight back, nice, deep, rounded hams. A clean chest and a neck that leaves the body in the right place, not dropping away as some pigs will. And she must have pretty eyes.'

Prize pigs need constant cleaning and each pig is meticulously washed more than a dozen times before show day. Ms Radbone favours Velvet soap for the washing as it won't bring a sensitive pig out in a rash. She scrubs her pigs with a soft brush and rinses them off in warm water, paying special attention to the ears and tail, and then dries them off in sawdust.

During winter, when the blowfly activity is at its lowest, legs from little pigs are salted, brined and hung in the chimney to smoke. Every day for the first three days, coarse sea salt and ground black pepper are massaged in. A pickle is made by bringing red wine, vinegar, salt, sugar, garlic, fresh thyme and bay leaves to the boil, and then letting the mixture cool.

The hams are bathed in this brine in an old slate wash-trough for twenty days. A rod hangs in the throat of the biggest chimney, well away from the fire, and on this the hams hang for a week or two. The fire is occasionally doused with oak chips collected from wine barrel shavings, or with branches of bay.

After smoking the hams are wrapped in muslin cloth and hung in the apple shed to air-dry. Attention is paid to the shank bone, as this is the first place flies strike. The hams are usually eaten or brought into the coolroom before Christmas, but can keep for a year or more.

Smaller cuts like bacon or spareribs can be dry-salted and may be smoked over woodchips in a small tin smoke-box sold in hardware shops. Paul Bocuse's *The New Cuisine* has a great recipe for ham poached in hay.

Janet Jeffs, South Australia

INDIVIDUAL STEAK AND KIDNEY PIES FROM THE HOUSE AT MOUNT PRIOR

THESE PIES are a favourite winter Sunday lunch for the guests at The House. They are made in small soufflé bowls and can be prepared well in advance.

1 kg gravy beef, well
trimmed
6 lamb's kidneys
some Bertolli light olive oil
for browning the meat
2 medium onions, finely
chopped
1/2 cup port
1/2 litre beef stock
1/4 teaspoon nutmeg
2 cloves garlic, crushed
salt and pepper to taste
a little cornflour (optional)
200 g puff pastry
1 egg
a little water

Dice the beef into bite-sized chunks and trim the kidneys of all fat and gristle. Put a fine layer of oil in a pan and when very hot brown the meat on all sides. Remove the meat and sauté the onions in the same pan until lightly browned. Deglaze the pan with the port and replace the beef. Toss in the kidneys, stir for a few minutes and then pour in the stock. Add the nutmeg and garlic and season with salt and pepper. Cover and cook over a gentle heat for 1 hour or until the meat is tender.

Drain the meat and distribute between 6 small oven-proof bowls. Thicken the juices in the pot with a little cornflour or reduce as desired and pour over the meat. Roll out the pastry and cut 6 circles of a size to cover and overlap the top of the soufflé bowls. Paint a line of egg wash (a yolk mixed with a little water) around the rim and when the meat is cool, press the pastry circles on top of the rim. Glaze with egg wash. Refrigerate for 30 minutes to rest the pastry.

Bake in a preheated oven at 190°C until the pastry is golden-brown. Serve with a selection of steamed vegetables and a crusty loaf to mop up the juices.

SERVES 6

Tricia Hennessy, Victoria

....

To keep meat juices *or glaze, pour into an earthenware*
pot and cover with clarified butter. If the fat layer is
airtight, the glaze or jellied stock will keep for weeks.

LAMB NECKS WITH DRIED BEANS AND FRESH VEGETABLES

A GOOD recipe for spring when lamb is at its most tender.

1 cup dried white beans
3 whole lamb necks, split
lengthways
90 g butter
2 leeks, trimmed and sliced
2 parsnips, cut into small
cubes
3 carrots, cut into small
cubes
small wine glass Cognac
few sprigs fresh thyme
3 fresh bay leaves
2 pieces dried orange peel
(optional)
140 g tomato paste
salt, sugar and pepper
parsley to garnish

Soak the beans in warm water and leave overnight. Drain. Trim as much fat as possible from the necks. Melt 60 g of the butter in a heavy pot and brown the meat on all sides. Remove from the pot and wipe it out. Add the rest of the butter to the pot and sauté the leeks, parsnips and carrots until softened. Pour in the Cognac. Replace the necks on top of the vegetables and pour in enough water to cover. Add the herbs, beans, orange peel and tomato paste. Season with salt, sugar and pepper and cover. Cook for 2-4 hours very slowly until the meat pulls easily off the bone.

Serve with hot buttered noodles. For variations, add to the broth, in season, asparagus tips, green beans, broad beans or peas.

SERVES 6

Penny Smith, Victoria

GENTLEMAN'S RELISH

500 g good steak (rump or
porterhouse)
125 g butter
a little grated nutmeg
black pepper
2 bay leaves (and a few
extra to garnish)
pinch cayenne
ghee
1 small tin anchovy fillets or
12 Bella dei Tindari
anchovy fillets from
Western Australia

Cut the steak into 3 or 4 pieces, removing any fat and gristle. Put the steak and all other ingredients, except the anchovies, into a basin. Cover with foil and tie securely. Steam for 2 hours or until tender.

Purée meat with the anchovies in a food processor to form a paste. Spoon into china pots. When cool, add a bay leaf to each pot and seal with ghee.

MAKES I CUP

Nellie Ramsay, Victoria

VINTNER'S GOURMET PIE FLOATER

THE PIE floater is a pastry dish peculiar to South Australia. Marjorie Coats has prepared her own version, infinitely better than the original, for the Barossa Gourmet Weekends. They have proved an enormous success.

'Pie floaters' first found their way onto the Adelaide streets about 80 years ago. Twelve-year-old Alf Trim was working in his stepfather's catering business, which consisted of a pie-cart drawn by one or sometimes two horses, selling their wares on the corner of King William and Rundle Streets in the city. At around 7.00 am it was Alf's job to go to the pie-cart, unhitch the horses and ride them bareback to the stables in Waymouth Street. He would then walk back to the pie-cart where he would be the 'washer and wiper upper' for Alexander, who ran the cart for Alf's stepfather. At 1.00 am, when the pie-cart closed, Alf would walk back to the stable, ride the horse back to the pie-cart (doing this twice if two horses were being used), and then head home at around 2.00 am.

One morning Alexander went to visit the toilet and Alf was left to mind the till. Along came a sailor who said, 'Give us a floater, sonny.' Alf had no idea what a floater was, so the sailor offered to show him. In those days there were no plastic plates or cups; the pies from Alf's cart were served on 'fantastic, wide, deep plates'. 'Give me that plate,' the sailor demanded. 'And pull a pie out.' (Pie-carts had a small wood stove which warmed the pies in the oven and heated the peas on top.) 'Put the pie in the middle of the plate, and ladle some peas over the top.' By now Alf thought he was dealing with a madman. The sailor then asked for the sauce, which he slopped all over the pie. 'Now that's what I call a floater, and don't you ever forget it, sonny.'

Until then the pie-cart had served pies, pasties and, in the habit of the English, plates of blue boiler peas. Alf would come home from school and have to boil the dark blue boiler peas in a big black iron pot. They were sold for twopence a bowl, with a little vinegar to add flavour. Pies and pasties were twopence and the sauce was a penny extra.

Alf began to serve quite a few 'floaters' and they became very popular. Two out of three customers would order a floater at five pence each. (Pasties were never sold as floaters.) As floaters were not available anywhere else in Australia, they became an Adelaide landmark and many other pie-carts began to serve them. In the 1930s it is estimated that 150 pie-carts plied their wares on the streets of Adelaide. There are still pie-carts in Adelaide, and the one outside the Casino has been operating since 1958. It is now run by Balfours.

Marjorie Coats's version of South Australia's own special dish follows. ▶

PASTRY

125 g plain flour
125 g self-raising flour
pinch salt
125 g butter
about 100 ml water

FILLING

1 kg topside steak
plain flour
2 large onions
olive oil
1.5 litres beef stock

PEA SOUP

1 smoked pork hock
6 litres water
2 large onions
500 g split green peas

Pastry: Sift flours and salt. Rub the butter in with your fingers until the mixture resembles breadcrumbs. Gradually add sufficient water to make a firm dough. Turn onto a floured board and knead lightly; do not handle too much as the pastry will toughen. Leave to rest in a cool place.

Filling: Trim any fat or gristle from the meat and cut into small cubes. Toss lightly in plain flour. Chop the onions into small dice. Cover the bottom of a pan with oil, sauté the onions, and add the meat, browning quickly. Add the stock. Bring to the boil and then reduce the heat and simmer until the meat is tender. Season to taste and leave to cool.

Soup: Cut slits in the pork hock and place in a large saucepan with the water. Peel and dice the onions and add to the water along with the peas. Bring to the boil, stirring occasionally. Allow to boil for approximately 2 hours or until the soup has reduced by half. Remove the hock and rub the soup through a sieve. Skin the hock and remove the meat from the hock bones. Chop the meat and return to the soup.

Roll out the pastry to ¼ cm thickness and cut out 6 pie tops to fit your moulds. Use the remaining pastry to line 6 greased pie moulds. Divide the meat mixture amongst the lined pie tins and brush the edges of the pastry with beaten egg. Place the pie tops on the dishes and press the edges together with a fork. Pierce the top of each pie with a knife and brush the tops with egg. Bake on a tray in the middle of the oven at 180°C until the pastry is cooked and golden. Allow to stand for a few minutes before turning out of tins.

To serve, place a hot pie in a large, warmed soup bowl. Ladle a generous serve of hot soup around the pie. Serve accompanied by tomato sauce and vinegar. The sauce is traditionally poured over the pie, but be careful to add only about half a teaspoonful of vinegar if desired.

Marjorie Coats, South Australia

PIGS' TROTTERS IN SWEET VINEGAR

'THE TRADITIONAL civilisations of China elevated dining to an art form, embellishing eating and drinking with charming ceremonial. The art of dining involves the application of the philosophy of Heaven, Earth and People.'

So says Dr F.T. Cheng in his Musings of a Chinese Gourmet. Yin and Yang are opposing forces that regulate the universe and all things: dark and light, weak and strong. And the Chinese people prepare dishes in accord with the nature of the purpose. The Western world does, too, to a certain extent, celebrating many occasions with traditional meals, but the Chinese go much further than that.

Before being able to appreciate Cheong Liew and his cooking, it is necessary to understand some of this Chinese philosophy and the orientation that is reflected in his food. For example, when Cheong's wife Mary was expecting their fourth child, it seemed perfectly natural to prepare the enriching and traditional dish that Cantonese and Fukenese women eat one month before giving birth. Pungent and tongue-burning chunks of mature ginger are baked in a large clay pot with pigs' trotters, swimming in a mahogany-coloured, rich, sweet and sour sauce. It is cooked for hours, until the trotters are rendered succulent and gelatinous.

Chinese mothers-in-law prepare this meal for their daughters-in-law, willing their offspring to be a boy. Nearer the birth of the baby, hard-boiled eggs are added and the mother is presented with a bowl as soon as possible after the baby is born. She is then expected to eat this dish three times a day. The Chinese believe this meal epitomises the Yin and Yang elements inside her body and that eating it is essential to her strength and well-being.

This dish improves with reheating. All the flavours infuse and become softer as the trotter jelly is released.

4 pigs' trotters
4 large roots fresh ginger
1 tablespoon sesame oil
375 ml sweet black vinegar
2 tablespoons rice wine
4 hard-boiled eggs

Singe the hair off the trotters over a gas flame and put the trotters into a large pot. Cover with water, bring to the boil and cook for 45 minutes. Peel the ginger roots and chop roughly. Stir-fry the ginger in a dry wok for a few minutes, then add the sesame oil.

Remove the trotters from their water and toss them in the wok long enough to become flavoured with the ginger. Put all the wok ingredients into a large clay pot. Pour on the vinegar, the wine and enough water to almost cover. Simmer gently for about 1½ hours. Sweeten with extra sugar if you like.

Cool and keep for 24 hours before reheating. Add the shelled hard-boiled eggs before serving.

Cheong Liew, South Australia

SUNDAY LUNCH

I REMEMBER Sunday mornings when, as the eldest son, I suffered the dubious privilege of accompanying my mother to the little wooden Presbyterian church up the road. I would console myself with the thought of the impending miracle of roast lunch. I worried that the Reverend Mr Reid was to be there—the table would be adorned with the best linen and that meant don't spill the beetroot. And the old family silver with the silver plate worn away made the mint sauce taste brassy.

Though I have a fair understanding of cooking, I'm still not sure why roasts from our old IXL stove tasted better. Maybe the 'two tooth' which grazed our spring pastures had something to do with it. None of the current-day 'Spring Lamb' propaganda would have worked on my father. Our 'killers', as he condemned them, were the pick of the flock and got special treatment, though I thought that was little compensation for their death sentence.

We had fresh fruit and vegies from our garden all year round, and also from there, plenty of worms for luring red fin or yella belly onto our hooks. Occasionally we caught Murray cod from the Goulburn River, which we would bake until the skin was crispy brown, and serve as great cod steaks with lemon juice, salt and pepper. The mashed potato was light and fluffy then, and seemed to absorb huge globs of cream and home-made butter without going to slop. Snowflake potatoes, they were called, difficult to peel because of the eyes.

I associate forequarter roasts most with harvest times, especially chaff cutting. When the clatter of the cutter shut down the kitchen would fill with the smell of hard work, drive-belt tar and axle grease. Your feet prickled with socks full of grass seeds and you boiled if you got the kitchen chair where you sat with your back to the stove.

Shearing time must have been a good time for our laying hens. Morning and afternoon 'smoko' meant blissful, hot silence, and scones piled with boiled eggs mashed with cream, plenty of pepper and salt and sometimes chopped parsley (though I preferred it without). Lunch was mother's egg and bacon pie, served cold with home-made tomato sauce; the tomatoes stung your lips with their acid.

The shearers had their own tea ceremony, I recall. They'd hang their billy on the water tank of the shearing plant engine, which was always boiling, then toss a big handful of tea into their chipped enamel mugs and top them up with water. That tea always had a rainbow on the surface from the oil that sputtered from the engine or the lanolin that was heavy in the air.

Outside of shearing time, our dogs used to practise their trade by rounding up the chooks—I suppose that's why the poultry tasted different to today's. A mixture of fear and exercise, along with the bounty from ceaseless foraging, gave them a flavour that, in my memory, sets them apart from today's 'free range' birds. Perhaps it was just our stove, or the fact that everything we ate was slightly tainted by the ever-smoking kerosene fridge and lamps.

Flour and sugar came in bags and honey and bees came in hives. Yorky Pell used to rob the hives for us and got to keep half the honey for his trouble. My father cleverly developed an allergy to bee stings. Yorky drank but my father didn't—he said as a young bloke he had fun without it. He did, and didn't need it to roll cars either, so people said. Thermos tea and Murray cray sandwiches were my father's weaknesses. We'd boil crays in the copper and the wash-house would smell for weeks after. Every scrap of meat was picked from the cray shells and then we feasted on the meat with salt and pepper as the only anointment for this heavenly luxury.

Rolled brisket of beef plucked from wooden tubs of pickling brine was another favourite. We always had young, whole buttered spuds, and cold beetroot and carrot and parsnip mashed together. Usually the greens were peas or gritty silverbeet. I preferred the peas, boiled in channel water with some sugar and salt. The pea water was mine, with a little milk and pepper.

Cheese didn't play a big role in out lives, except for macaroni cheese in white sauce. Two other uses for macaroni were making necklaces and eating it baked with a sweet, cheeseless custard.

Offal was really my father's and my favourite. We loved tripe in white sauce with onions, brain fritters or brain in sandwiches, mashed with cream. Kidneys and liver cooked in any fashion were devoured with gusto. We shared poultry giblets, stewed for breakfast. We even used to peel the chooks' feet and boil them with other edible innards, thickening the juice with cornflour. I can smell it still, even though it's thirty years since I ate that dish.

I don't really have a sweet tooth, but my mouth waters at the thought of golden syrup dumplings or steamed pud. We used to cook dumplings in our Namco pressure cooker until us kids lost the weight off the top of it and it wouldn't seal. This made the dumplings lighter and fluffier or something, though I forget exactly. Another newfangled gadget we had was a jaffle iron. It was cast iron, black, and heavy as hell. An after-school feed was jaffles filled with grated apple or a whole egg with bacon. Nowadays they serve jaffles for breakfast at the Yarra Bend public golf course. It's the only thing that makes me persist with my game.

Perhaps it's just that I look at food these days with older, more sentimental eyes. Maybe I taste it with a jaded palate, but still, the special meat I ate last week doesn't hold that same flavour as the meat down on the farm. I still comb the menu looking for cold meat fritters, shepherd's pie or lamb's fry with bacon, and golden syrup dumplings to follow. Funny, isn't it?

Richard Thomas,
Victoria

ROAST LOIN OF PORK WITH MUSTARD AND REDCURRANT GLAZE

ACCORDING to Jane Grigson, the secret of cooking fresh pork is salting the meat for a clear 12 hours before roasting.

1 loin of pork, boned, with
flap and skin left on
500 g Granny Smith apples
1 small tin black truffles
4 tablespoons redcurrant
jelly
2 teaspoons Keens English
mustard
¹/₂ cup veal or chicken stock
¹/₂ cup port

BRINE
12 cups water
375 g sea salt
375 g soft brown sugar
1 teaspoon juniper berries
¹/₄ teaspoon nutmeg
bay leaf
3 sprigs fresh thyme
1 teaspoon black
peppercorns
4 cloves

To prepare the brine, put the water, salt and sugar into a large pot and bring it to the boil. Tie the berries, herbs and spices in a muslin bag and add to the pot. Allow to cool.

Remove all the rind from the pork in one piece and trim off as much fat as possible. Place the meat in the cold brine and leave for 12 hours.

Slice the truffles, reserving the juice. Peel and core the apples. Stew apples gently until soft and then purée. Drain off excess juice and set aside. Season the inside of the loin flap and spread on the purée. Add truffle slices, roll up flap and tie the rind back around the loin.

Bake on a rack at 175°C for 45 minutes, adding water to the pan with the drippings. Remove from the oven and untie the crackling. Combine the redcurrant jelly and mustard, and glaze the loin with this mixture. Turn the oven temperature up to hot and cook for a further 30 minutes.

Slice off any fat from the crackling. Cut the crackling into serving portions. Sprinkle with water and salt and continue cooking until crisp. Rest the meat for 10 minutes before carving.

Strain the pan juices into a pot, add the stock, port, reserved apple and truffle juices and reduce to a sauce consistency. Season before serving.

SERVES 6

Melinda Waters, Victoria

RABBIT CASSEROLE

'ENTIRELY ORGANIC' was Jane and Jimmy Barnes's only specification to Denis King who devised their vegetable garden. The result looks inviting and is easy to move around in with a wheelbarrow and mower.

The slope of the land meant terracing—railway sleepers provide the required depth of soil for growing root vegetables, and are perfect for constructing steps and walkways between the plots. Picket fences keep out the dogs and there is a herb garden right along the front. The soil is a mixture of about 70 per cent mushroom compost, 20 per cent compost from their own compost heap and the remainder sharp washed river sand. Chicken manure (dynamic lifter) is added to the soil with each new crop.

No chemicals have ever been used to control pests and diseases. Crops are rotated with each planting; crops from the same family are never planted in the same plot in succession. Actively growing healthy plants fend for themselves when it comes to the occasional insect attack, and they always outgrow the problem, according to Denis: 'I purposely split the crops—a row of lettuce here, another a few plots away—to make it as difficult as possible for the bugs to find them. I also interplant the various plots with rows of onions and shallots, which I think contributes to keeping the insects away.

'So far we've had no problems with the garden. We have produced peas, beans, corn, cauliflower, broccoli, strawberries, spinach, chillies, onions, tomatoes, squash, zucchini, parsley, lettuce and many oriental vegetables. The herb garden includes sage, thyme, five varieties of mint, horseradish, coriander, dill, marjoram, oregano, cress, lemon balm and others according to the season. The crops have been very successful—the produce is larger and tastier than store-bought vegetables and free of pests, diseases and chemicals.'

Of the following recipe, Jimmy says: 'Any herbs can be substituted; these particular three worked well. I find that picking different herbs, rubbing them together and smelling the combination is the best way to judge how much and what to use. The quantities in the ingredients do not really matter and can vary according to the cook. In fact, everything in the recipe can vary. The way to success with this dish is to cook by feel and taste and not by rigidly sticking to the measurements.' ▶

For the best pork crackling, *dry the skin thoroughly, brush the scored skin with vinegar and sprinkle with salt before cooking for 20 minutes in a hot oven.*

1 rabbit
2 Spanish onions, roughly
  chopped
olive oil
6 cloves garlic
3 potatoes, diced
3 carrots, diced
8 baby turnips, diced
250 ml water
⅓ bottle dry white wine
1 x 100 g jar tomato paste
salt and pepper
Maggi seasoning sauce
winter savoury, sage, Italian
  parsley

Separate the rabbit into average-sized pieces. Brown the onions in olive oil. Crush in the garlic. Throw in the rabbit and seal, slightly browning it. Add the vegetables and fry for a few minutes. Transfer all to a baking dish and add the water, wine, tomato paste, salt, pepper, Maggi sauce and herbs. Give the stew a good stir, cover and bake in the oven at 180°C for a minimum of 2 hours. Check and stir now and then.

Serve with wild rice and green beans. It is even better eaten the next day.

SERVES 4

Jimmy Barnes, New South Wales

....

Marinate pork *fillet in a mixture of 1 tablespoon dry sherry, 2 tablespoons honey, 1 teaspoon salt, 1 tablespoon soy sauce and 1 tablespoon hoi sin sauce for 24 hours. Roast for 20 minutes at 190°C to make Chinese roasted pork or cha sui. It is delicious cut up and added to fried rice or salads.*

Soak wooden skewers *in water overnight before using for satay or shashlik. It is easier to thread on the meat and it helps prevent the sticks from burning.*

◇ ◇ ◇ NOTES ◇ ◇ ◇

Use your electric blender *to chop fresh ginger and garlic with a little vinegar or sherry to moisten. Several weeks' supply can be processed at once. Stored in a sealed jar in the refrigerator—it will keep indefinitely.*

Desserts & Sweets

· · · · · · · · · · · · · ·

APPLE CHARLOTTES

4 large Granny Smith apples
2 heaped tablespoons sugar
   (or more to suit taste)
squeeze lemon juice
cloves or cinnamon to taste
thinly sliced bread
melted butter

Core, peel and slice the apples and put in a saucepan with the sugar, lemon juice and spices. Cook, covered, for 5 minutes so that the apple begins cooking in its own juices, then remove lid and cook until all liquid is driven off. The apple must be very thick—any liquid will cause the finished charlottes to collapse.

Line 4 dariole moulds with bread which has been dipped in melted butter on both sides. Start by cutting circles to fit the tops of the moulds, then line the sides, making sure of a very tight fit. Spoon the apple mixture into the centre and tap on the bench to make sure the filling settles.

Bake at 200°C for 30 minutes or until crust is golden-brown. Turn onto individual serving plates and serve at once with any one of the following sauces: crème anglaise flavoured with Calvados; apricot sauce (soak and cook dried apricots, then purée and sweeten); plum sauce.

SERVES 4

Wyn Drabble, New Zealand

BERRY COMPOTE

3 tablespoons sugar
1/2 cup water
3 punnets berries (e.g.
   strawberries, blueberries
   or blackberries)
1 tablespoon lemon juice

Heat sugar and water in a heavy pan and stir until dissolved. If using strawberries, halve and hull them. Add the lemon juice and berries to the pan and cook gently for no more than 2 or 3 minutes, shaking the pan gently to coat the berries with the syrup. Spoon the berries next to a thin slice of chocolate cake and dust with icing sugar.

Jill Dupleix, Victoria

BLACK RICE AND PALM SUGAR CUSTARD

You will need 4 dariole moulds or a 4-cup oblong cake tin.

125 g (¹/₂ cup) sugar
125 g (¹/₂ cup) black rice
(palm sugar and black
rice readily available in
Vietnamese food shops)
220 g (1³/₄ cups) palm sugar
500 ml (2 cups) milk
5 eggs

In a heavy metal pan melt the sugar over a gentle heat to a light toffee colour. Pour equal amounts into each mould. Wash, soak and cook the rice according to the instructions on the packet and put 2 tablespoons into the bottom of each mould.

Bring the milk to the boil, remove from the heat and add the crumbled palm sugar. Stir until dissolved. Beat the eggs lightly and stir into the sugar and milk. Strain this mixture equally into the moulds. Put the moulds into a steamer and cook gently until the custard is just set to touch (approximately 30 minutes). Refrigerate for 24 hours and invert onto serving plates.

SERVES 4

Cheong Liew, South Australia

CARDAMOM ICE-CREAM

6 egg yolks
3 whole eggs
10 g cardamom seed, lightly
ground
200 g castor sugar
600 ml cream, whipped to a
medium peak
6 egg whites

Whisk egg yolks, whole eggs, cardamom and half the sugar over a water bath until the mixture is very thick and reaches ribbon stage. Beat over cold water until cool. Fold in the whipped cream.

Whisk egg whites with the rest of the sugar and fold gently into the egg and cream mixture. Freeze. Take out of the freezer about half an hour before serving. Makes about 2.5 litres.

Janet Jeffs, South Australia

Boysenberries are *a cross between blackberries and raspberries. They were developed by Rudolph Boysen in 1923.*

BREAD AND BUTTER PUDDING WITH PEACHES

BREAD AND BUTTER Toffee Pudding was served at Blind Creek one evening when I was a dinner guest. Jane Grimwade and her family have run a bed-and-breakfast business in Benalla for some time. The dessert was so good I asked her to share the recipe.

6 fresh, ripe peaches
45 g butter, softened
12 slices white bread, crusts removed
3 teaspoons cinnamon

TOFFEE
3/4 cup sugar
3/4 cup water

CUSTARD
3 eggs
140 g castor sugar
1 cup milk, scalded
1 cup cream, scalded
2 tablespoons Benedictine

Firstly prepare the toffee. Put the sugar and water in a pan and stir over a low heat until the sugar dissolves. Increase the heat and cook until the toffee is a golden colour. Pour into a buttered 25 cm round, ovenproof dish.

Poach the peaches in water until just tender. Drain and slice. Butter the bread on one side and cut into triangles. Cover the toffee base with the bread, buttered side down.

To make the custard, put the eggs and sugar into a bowl and whisk, then beat in the scalded milk, cream and liqueur.

Cover the bread triangles with sliced peaches and scatter on some cinnamon. Repeat these layers until all the bread, peaches and cinnamon have been used up. Then pour on the custard carefully and allow to stand for several minutes.

Place the pudding in a water bath and bake at 180°C for 50-60 minutes or until the custard is set. Allow to stand for 10 minutes before turning out to serve.

SERVES 6

Jane Grimwade, Victoria

If custard curdles, *remove it from the heat and add a little cold water. Whisk hard with a beater and your custard should return to its satiny smoothness.*

GOAT'S CHEESE AND FRESH DATE TART

PASTRY
185 g flour
90 g butter
salt
1 tablespoon iced water
watercress to garnish

FILLING
10 fresh dates
2 logs fresh goat's cheese
2 eggs
100 ml crème fraîche
salt and pepper
1 bunch fresh lemon thyme

Pastry: Put the flour and butter into the food procesor with a good pinch of salt. Process until the mixture resembles breadcrumbs. Add the chilled water and process again until the mixture 'balls'. Remove the dough to a marble slab and roll out thinly, to cover a rectangular or oblong tart tin with a removable base. Prick the pastry base thoroughly and put it into the freezer for at least 30 minutes. (You may prepare this the day before.)

Preheat the oven to 175°C and bake the tart base straight from the freezer, until golden. Set aside to cool.

Filling: Cut the dates in half and remove the stone. Cut the cheese into thin rounds. Combine the eggs and crème fraîche in a bowl (if it is too thick add a little water). Arrange the dates and cheese slices interlacing over the pre-cooked tart base. Pour on the custard and scatter on a generous amount of lemon thyme leaves. Return to the oven and bake at 175°C until the custard has set. Brown the top under the grill a little before serving warm with a sprig of watercress or thyme.

SERVES 8

Penny Smith, Victoria

DINEY RAINSFORD'S HARD SAUCE

60 g (3 tablespoons) butter
20 ml (1 tablespoon) boiling water
135 g (³⁄₄ cup) icing sugar
20 ml (1 tablespoon) sherry or brandy

Cream all the ingredients and spoon into a serving bowl. Dust the top with freshly grated nutmeg and then chill.

Nan Mann, PWMU Cookbook

GOOSEBERRY TART

THIS IS one of the most exquisite fruit tarts I have ever eaten. Prepare the pastry the day before. The recipe is from the Auberge of the Flowering Hearth.

TART BASE
7 g (1 sachet) dried yeast
125 ml warm milk
250 g flour
4 tablespoons sugar
pinch salt
135 g butter
2 eggs
2 teaspoons water
1 egg yolk and 1 tablespoon
* milk, for glazing*

FILLING
1 kg gooseberries, trimmed
875 g sugar

Base: Stir the yeast into the warm milk. Sift the flour, sugar and salt together into a large bowl and add the butter chopped into small pieces. Lightly beat the milk/yeast mixture, eggs and water and add to the centre of the flour. Work to a very sticky dough (this is easily done in a food processor). Form the pastry into a ball. Cover and keep warm (20-25°C). Allow to rise for 3 hours. Punch down, roll into a ball and refrigerate overnight.

About 2½ hours before serving, roll out the chilled dough to fit a buttered 25 cm flan tin. Leave to rise for another 2 hours. Preheat oven to 220°C. When the dough has risen, cover with holed foil, fill with dried beans and bake blind for 10 minutes. Lower the temperature, brush the rim of the shell with glaze and bake a further 5-10 minutes. Remove the foil and beans 5 minutes before the shell is cooked. Cool.

Filling: Put the gooseberries into a pan with the sugar. Stir over gentle heat until they split. When the juice turns to syrup, remove the gooseberries with a slotted spoon. Increase the heat and boil until thickened.

Cover the cooked base with gooseberries and pour on the hot syrup. As it cools the syrup becomes jelly.

SERVES 6-8

Jennifer Hillier, South Australia

....

To keep *the summer bounty of berries, spread them out on a baking sheet and freeze. When frozen, pack them into containers—this way they hold their shape.*

GRAN ALLEN'S CHRISTMAS PUDDING

GRAN ALLEN was my sister's mother-in-law. Nobody knows where she got this recipe but when our children were little she used to make this pudding and bring it with her on Christmas Day. I think it is my favourite pudding recipe, and we have now been making it for many years. It has become a family tradition, a legacy left to us from Gran Allen who has been dead for many years.

250 g raisins
250 g currants
375 g sultanas
125 g dates, chopped
60 g mixed peel
60 g cherries, sliced
1 small apple, peeled and
    grated
grated rind of 1 orange
1 wineglass brandy
strained juice and grated
    rind of 1 lemon
250 g soft unsalted butter
250 g soft brown sugar
5 x 60 g eggs
1 tablespoon treacle
250 g flour
$\frac{1}{2}$ teaspoon salt
$\frac{1}{2}$ teaspoon ground ginger
1 teaspoon nutmeg
1 teaspoon mixed spice
250 g soft white
    breadcrumbs
60 g blanched almonds
1 extra wineglass brandy

Soak all fruit and rind in brandy and lemon juice overnight. Cream butter and sugar. Add eggs, beating well after each addition. Fold in treacle. Sift flour, salt and spices and fold carefully into creamed butter mixture. Combine breadcrumbs with brandied fruit and carefully fold both mixtures, a spoonful at a time. Add the almonds last.

Butter a large pudding basin and spoon the mixture into it. Cover the basin tightly with 2 layers of buttered tough brown paper. Cover with foil and tie with string. Steam the pudding very gently for 4 hours. Cool and store in a dark place.

On Christmas Day: Steam for approximately $\frac{3}{4}$ hour. Unmould, pour over a wineglass of warm brandy and ignite.

SERVES 8

Penny Smith, Victoria

To frost grapes, *wash and dry them thoroughly, and cut into clusters. Beat 2 egg whites lightly with a silver fork—do not make them froth. Sift castor sugar onto a sheet of paper. Brush the grapes with the egg white and dip them into the sugar. Allow them to dry on a rack.*

GRAND MARNIER WAFFLES FROM THE HOUSE AT MOUNT PRIOR

TRICIA HENNESSY and I spend hours in the kitchen cooking together. The House at Mount Prior has become a second home and I have got to know the kitchen intimately with all its treasures. The fridge, freezer and pantry are always crammed with ingredients waiting for me to create: meat glaze and wobbly stock, fruit purée and home-made ice-creams, smelly cheeses, and produce fresh from the orchard garden.

Tricia and I work well together under pressure or just cooking shared ideas for the pleasure of it. She can cook for large numbers at the drop of a hat. She makes wonderful bread in Swiss roll tins (see page 112), serving it with home-made pâté or terrine. She bakes lamb shanks in the oven until the meat is almost liquid and the gelatinous juices coat your palate with a richness that needs a good swig of blackberry coloured durif, a red wine from the cellars of the House, to compete. She makes steak and kidney pies with sophistication and serves them with country warmth and generosity. Her food can be complicated or simple but it is always beautifully presented—like the light and airy waffles, made from eggs warm from the chooks and garnished with Grand Marnier butter, which are served to me in bed with champagne and the weekend papers. What luxury and how special!

When staying in the Champagne Suite I wake to the birds and the vineyards stretch before me. The sun usually streams through the window and the day starts with fresh air and kitchen smells. Tricia works to prepare the feasts for another onslaught of guests. I join her eventually and we share the tasks with laughter and enthusiasm. The pace can be hot or relaxed—it doesn't matter. We work in harmony. There are few I can share so much with or who are so generous with their knowledge and space.

WAFFLES
125 g butter
½ cup sugar
3 eggs
½ cup plain flour
1 cup self-raising flour
pinch of cinnamon
400 ml milk
good dash Grand Marnier

Cream the butter and sugar and add the eggs. Sift the flours and cinnamon, then add alternately with the milk. Lastly, flavour with the liqueur. Set aside for 30 minutes before cooking. Tricia uses an electronically controlled waffle pan.

BUTTER
125 g unsalted butter
¼ cup castor sugar
zest of 1 orange
good dash Grand Marnier
icing sugar

Cream all the ingredients and chill in a pot until firm. Spoon onto the hot waffles so that the butter melts and oozes. Dust with icing sugar.

Tricia Hennessy, Victoria

$\mathcal{H}$ ONEYFLOW HOMESTEAD

I HAVE journeyed by car a couple of times up the Newell Highway and on to Far North Queensland. Every town you pass through has its own tourist information bureau and I always check to see what is advertised in the area. The bureaus are staffed by volunteers who are enthusiastic and willing to help you explore the surrounding area. However nothing I had read prepared me for Honeyflow Homestead.

Hard to find, on the Atherton Tablelands, this old Queenslander is set in a small pocket of rainforest that is home to the rare tree kangaroo. These nocturnal animals live high in the canopy of the forest and are extremely shy. I spent hours with a halogen torch searching the leafy branches, until the rain drove us home to bed cold and disappointed.

Before dawn the next day we awoke to mugs of tea and a short walk to a nearby waterway. Sitting silent and still on the bank, we were rewarded with seven platypuses swimming and feeding, unconcerned with our presence. How rare to see them at such close quarters. We stayed until the sun rose and it was time to feed ourselves, on home-made bread and swamp mahogany honey.

Honey is an all-purpose natural sweetener which gives energy. It should be stored in a dry place as it absorbs moisture. Refrigeration hastens granulation, but this does not affect the purity of the honey. To re-liquefy it, place it in a container of warm (not hot) water. (If it is overheated the colour and flavour will be spoilt.) When baking cakes and biscuits, add the honey in a fine stream. Honey adds to the keeping quality of all baked foods.

The owners of Honeyflow Homestead are Ron and Judy English. Ron writes:

'I bought my first swarm of bees when I was a kid. I took it home in my hand cart and transferred it to a box. I didn't know any better then, but I know as much about bees as anybody now. I wasn't a big bee-keeper—I only had three to four hundred hives. Big keepers talk in thousands.

'To begin your bee-keeping you have to buy a queen from a breeder. The breeder might have up to 50 000 bees, selling them at a dollar a bee all over the world. The queens are bred for docility and disease resistance. There are various breeds—we use Caucasian bees from the Mediterranean, as they suit our climate. We buy pre-fabricated hives in kit form from a factory. We construct the hives and then put our own boxes inside, starting off what we call a 'nucleus colony' by taking a couple of frames to a new queen. Bee-keeping is one of the few industries where you can change breed within a couple of months by replacing a queen. With cattle it takes half a century.

'We used to pollinate crops for farmers by carting bees out to the farms and charging a dollar per hive per day. Then we would collect the honey. Honeyflow comes from a superabundance of flowering trees, and it is the bee-keeper's job to keep the bees on a honeyflow: as fast as they harvest one crop you have to take them to another. As the forests are cleared and pushed further back the harvesting becomes more difficult. At one time up here, you could see 4000 hectares of one species of tree and you could put your bees in the middle of them.

'Honey is like jam in that it derives its flavour from the nectar of a particular tree or plant. We discovered that rainforest has a very unusual flavour. The honey you buy in the shops is blended by the Marketing Board to a uniform colour and flavour. We went in for the exotics, getting honey from the sarsaparilla, macadamia, avocado and swamp mahogany trees.

'A bee-keeper has to be a very keen botanist, for nectar is the bee's carbohydrate and pollen is its protein source. Bees have to have a balanced diet and certain species of plants have only an abundant amount of one or the other. When bees have the correct diet they are remarkably efficient, filling a 27 kg box in a fortnight. Then you have to move them.

'We used to cover many different angles on our farm. We had a retail shop, a tasting bar and a bee-keeping display, and we used to pollinate for the local farmers. One day I put my bees onto an avocado orchard and got a bumper crop of almost black honey. 'What on earth will I do with it?' I thought. 'It's much too dark for the Board.' I sold it to a bloke who works the flea markets. One day I was hanging round the market when I read a sign: 'RARE AVOCADO HONEY'. He was selling it at a premium price! That was the last avocado honey I ever sold cheap. I kept it all and flogged it myself.

'World heritage listing of the forests has gone against the bee-keeper. Conservationists reckon the bees are keeping pollen from the parrots, tyre tracks are not allowed in the forest, and it is all too hard. As soon as you send your honey to market the Board downgrades it, so you don't even get the dol-lar per kilo they pay for 'choice' honey. The high cost of fuel and the fact that we haven't had a price rise for 15 years makes it all uneconomical—so now we run Honeyflow Settlers Cottage as a guest house. The homestead was built by the Heidke family in 1918 on the Atherton Tablelands. We have brought up our own kids here and now we run it with our own genuine hospitality, away from other people and telephones.'

HONEYFRUIT COBBLER

¹/₂ cup raw sugar
2 tablespoons butter
1 egg
¹/₂ cup milk
1 cup self-raising flour
pinch salt
1 teaspoon vanilla
1 cup sliced stoned fruit
100 ml honey
1 cup boiling water

Cream the raw sugar with 1 tablespoon of the butter. Add the egg and beat well. Stir in the milk. Sift together the flour and salt and add to the creamed mixture. Beat until smooth. Stir in the vanilla and then spread the batter evenly over the bottom of a buttered 20 cm square tin.

Put the fruit into a bowl. Stir the honey, boiling water and remaining butter together and pour this over the fruit. Spoon this mixture on top of the batter. Bake at 190°C for 45 minutes. Serve warm with custard or cream.

SERVES 4

Ron and Judy English, Queensland

....
When making custard *with custard powder, boil the sugar in with the milk and the saucepan will be much easier to wash.*

JELLY OF FRESH RASPBERRIES AND MINT CREAM

250 g sugar
250 ml water
4 sprigs fresh mint
1 dessertspoon Framboise
1 tablespoon lemon juice
3 rounded teaspoons
    gelatine powder
2 tablespoons water
500 g raspberries

MINT CREAM
about 15 mint leaves
1 tablespoon lemon juice
250 ml cream
30 mint leaves and a few
    perfect raspberries to
    decorate

Make a syrup by bringing sugar, water and mint leaves slowly to the boil. Simmer for a few minutes and allow to cool. Add Framboise and lemon juice.

Meanwhile, line 6 moulds with plastic wrap. Sponge the gelatine in the water, then place the bowl in a pan of simmering water until the gelatine has completely dissolved.

Remove the mint leaves from the syrup. Pour the syrup onto the gelatine and then add the raspberries. Fill the lined moulds. Leave to set in the refrigerator for 3-4 hours.

Mint Cream: Crush the mint leaves in a mortar and pestle with the lemon juice. Add the cream and stir. The lemon juice will thicken the cream; if it becomes too thick, add a little water.

To assemble: Spread a little mint cream on a white plate, turn out a raspberry jelly and place it in the centre. Arrange 5 mint leaves on the mint cream around the jelly. Decorate with a few perfect raspberries. Serve chilled.

MAKES 6 RAMEKINS

Rory O'Connell, Ireland

In France *in the early fourteenth century, people used to gather the tiny wild berries they found in the woods and forests. They transplanted the wild plants to their gardens. Strawberries* (Fragaria vesca) *became so popular that they have been specially propagated ever since to increase their size. Both the leaves and the berries are edible. Rich in vitamin C and iron, they were a popular food crop for the cottage garden.*

NAVEL ORANGES WITH ALMONDS AND VIOLETS

250 g (1 cup) almonds in
    their skins
250 ml (1 cup) milk
16 Navel oranges (2 per
    person)
40 ml (2 tablespoons) kirsch
250 g (1 cup) sugar
250 ml (½ cup) water
300 ml (1¼ cups) cream,
    whipped
16 fresh violets

Pour boiling water over the almonds and allow to cool. Slip off their skins, cover with the milk and set aside. Peel the oranges, removing all the segments with a sharp knife and leaving the membrane. Put into a bowl with the kirsch. Cover and chill.

Make a toffee by dissolving the sugar in the water over a gentle heat. As soon as the liquid begins to boil, without stirring again, allow it to colour to a rich brown. Pour this onto the oranges and set aside.

Before serving, rinse the milk off the almonds and stir them into the oranges. Spoon some oranges and their juice onto glass serving plates. Add a dollop of whipped cream and the petals of 2 violets.

SERVES 8

Penny Smith, Victoria

NECTARINE TART

pâte brisée to line a deep
    22 cm pie dish (see p. 93)
1 egg white or a little melted
    apricot jam
nectarines
150 g butter
200 g castor sugar
200 g unsalted macadamia
    nuts
3 eggs
75 ml Cognac or Cointreau

Prepare the pastry and bake it blind in a 200°C oven for 12 minutes. Turn down the heat to 180°C and bake a further 15 minutes. Paint the bottom of the pastry shell with beaten egg white or melted apricot jam. Allow to cool.

Slice the nectarines and arrange them decoratively in the pie shell. Cream the butter and sugar until fluffy. Pulverise ¾ of the macadamia nuts and add to the creamed mixture. Add the eggs one at a time, beating well after each addition, then the liqueur. Chop the remaining nuts roughly and fold them into the mixture.

Pour the batter over the nectarines and bake at 160°C for 1 hour or until the filling is set. Turn off the heat and allow the pie to cool in the oven. Serve with King Island Cream.

SERVES 6

Marieke Brugman, Victoria

OLD-FASHIONED RHUBARB TART

185 g (³/4 cup) plain flour
60 g (¹/4 cup) self-raising
*   flour*
salt
185 g (³/4 cup) unsalted
*   butter*
1 egg yolk
water
5-6 stalks rhubarb
juice of 1 large lemon
castor sugar
1 lightly beaten egg white

Sift the flours and salt together. Cut the butter into small pieces and rub it into the flour mixture with your fingers to resemble breadcrumbs. Mix the egg yolk with a little water and mix it into the flour until the mixture holds together. Pat into a cushion shape and freeze for 30 minutes while you prepare the rhubarb.

Chop the rhubarb into small pieces. Put it into a saucepan to cook with the lemon juice (this will preserve a good colour and improve the flavour). When tender, add sugar to your taste and allow to cool.

Roll out the pastry, leaving enough to make lattice strips, and line a 23 cm tart tin with removable base. Put it back into the refrigerator for 30 minutes. Line the tart case with foil and fill with rice. Bake blind in a moderate oven until coloured on the edges. Remove the foil and fill the centre with the cooled rhubarb.

Roll out the reserved pastry and cut decoratively into strips. Arrange in a criss-cross pattern on the top of the tart. Brush with egg white and dust with castor sugar. Bake in the oven for a further 15 minutes. Serve with fresh cream.

SERVES 4

Marie Popperwell, England

Add an apple *quarter and a cinnamon stick or clove to rhubarb when cooking for extra flavour.*

ORANGE AND CAMPARI JELLY

11 g or 1 sachet gelatine
350 ml clear apple juice
1 tablespoon Campari
2 oranges, segmented
    (reserve 8 segments for
    garnish)
4 stalks mint

Sprinkle the gelatine over the apple juice and Campari in a clean saucepan. Heat gently, but do not boil. Stir the mixture until clear and the gelatine has dissolved. Cool.

Pour a little jelly into 4 individual moulds and refrigerate until firm. When the jelly has set, remove from the refrigerator and arrange a mint leaf face down on top of the jelly, then an orange segment or two. Carefully pour on more jelly and refrigerate until set. Repeat this process until all the orange segments have been used and are completely covered with jelly. Fill the mould to the brim with jelly and chill until firmly set.

To unmould, dip the little moulds into tepid water and invert onto serving plates. Garnish with a sprig of mint and serve with a sauce of your choice. The jelly should not be too firm, so leave at room temperature to soften a little before serving.

SERVES 4

Lyn Hall, London

PÂTE BRISÉE

250 g flour
pinch salt
125 g chilled butter, diced
60-90 ml iced water

Sift the flour and salt together. Add the diced butter, gently rubbing it in with your fingertips. When evenly mixed, add the water—just enough to bind—and pat the dough into shape. Rest for 30 minutes. Roll out the pastry and line your desired tin. Prick the base thoroughly and refrigerate for 30 minutes.

Penny Smith, Victoria

PLUM PUDDING ICE-CREAM

250 g sugar
6 egg yolks
600 ml cream
2 teaspoons ground allspice
2 cinnamon sticks
1 split vanilla bean
185 g each raisins, sultanas
    and currants
60 g glacé cherries, chopped
grated rind of 1 orange and
    1 lemon
at least 1/2 cup Armagnac
125 g toasted slivered
    almonds
125 g grated dark bitter
    chocolate

Beat the sugar with the egg yolks until creamy. Put the cream into a pan with the allspice, cinnamon sticks and vanilla bean. Bring to the boil slowly and simmer for a few minutes. Turn off the heat and let stand for 30 minutes. Reheat the cream and strain it hot onto the beaten eggs. Cool and churn then put in the freezer. This may be done well ahead.

Put the raisins, sultanas, currants, cherries and grated rinds into a bowl. Pour on the Armagnac and leave to soak for 30 minutes. Remove the ice-cream from the freezer and allow to soften, then fold in the fruits with any liquid, the almonds and the chocolate. Pile the ice-cream back into the container and refreeze. If you wish, the ice-cream can be frozen in tiny pudding-shaped moulds and decorated with holly before serving.

Penny Smith, Victoria

ROSE PETAL CREAM

THIS WAS a delicious cream mould made to accompany fresh fruit for breakfast. It was served out of doors one beautiful January morning at The Hermitage in Great Western. It is equally good as a dessert.

300 ml cream
1 1/2 tablespoons gelatine
4 tablespoons water
2 large eggs, separated
60 g castor sugar
300 ml Greek yoghurt
2 tablespoons rose water
rose petals to decorate

Whip the cream. Dissolve the gelatine by putting it into a small bowl with the water and stirring over gentle heat. Beat the egg yolks and sugar until pale then fold in the yoghurt. Beat the whites to form soft peaks. Fold the cooled gelatine into the egg yolk mixture, adding the rose water, cream and lastly the beaten egg whites. Set in a fluted mould in the refrigerator. Turn out onto a serving plate, decorate with rose petals and serve with fresh fruit of your choice.

Sandra O'Malley, Victoria

QUINCE ICE-CREAM

1 litre water
1 kg sugar
1 vanilla pod, split
3 quinces
2 strips lemon rind and some
*   juice*
1 packet Dr Oetker sheet
*   gelatine*
600 ml cream, whipped

The day before, boil the sugar and water, stirring well. Add the vanilla pod. Peel and quarter the quinces and remove the cores. Place the quince pieces, skins and lemon rind in a muslin bag. Place in the syrup and bring to the boil. Transfer the pot to a 140°C/300°F oven for 2–3 hours. With slow cooking the quinces become tender and a deep cornelian colour. When the fruit is cooked and cooled, purée until smooth. Force the purée through a sieve, moistening with a little syrup to produce a thick liquid. Adjust the sweetness with lemon juice.

For each 750 ml of purée allow 6 leaves of gelatine (10 g powdered gelatine) and 600 ml cream, to yield 8 glasses or timbale moulds. (Your excess purée may be frozen.) Soak the leaf gelatine in cold water for 5 minutes and squeeze out the water. Put a third of the hot purée into a bowl and stir in the wet gelatine. When it has completely dissolved, fold in the rest of the fruit purée and allow to cool, whisking from time to time (to speed up the process put the bowl over ice). When it begins to set and leaves a thread falling from the whisk, fold in the whipped cream.

Lightly oil and dust the moulds with icing sugar. Pour in the quince cream and refrigerate for 6 hours before serving. Cinnamon Thins from *Jane Grigson's Fruit Book* (Michael Joseph 1982) make the perfect accompaniment.

Note: The poaching syrup may be reduced to make jelly using jam-making technique. It should reach 105°C to set. Strain through a muslin cloth and pour into jars. Add a strip of pithless lemon peel on top.

SERVES 8

Damien Pignolet, New South Wales

SAGO PLUM PUDDING

A SUBSITUTE pudding for Christmas.

4 tablespoons sago
2 cups milk
4 tablespoons melted butter
2 cups very stale
    breadcrumbs
2 cups raisins
1¹/₂ cups sugar
1 tablespoon finely chopped
    crystalised ginger
2 teaspoons bicarbonate of
    soda

Soak the sago in the milk overnight. Stir the melted butter into the breadcrumbs, then add the raisins, sugar, ginger and bicarbonate of soda. Mix thoroughly and if the mixture is too thick, add a little milk. Butter a basin and spoon in the mixture. Cover with buttered paper and foil, and fabric if you like, then tie it to seal as tightly as possible. Steam for 4 hours, making sure there is enough water in the pot to boil gently. Reheat on Christmas Day and serve with brandy butter.

BRANDY BUTTER SAUCE

3 cups water
3 tablespoons golden syrup
20 g sugar
2 tablespoons butter
2 tablespoons custard
    powder
2 tablespoons brandy

Combine all ingredients in a saucepan. Stir over a gentle heat with a whisk until thickened. This sauce reheats well.

Dulce Bell, Victoria

When making fruit ice-creams *or sorbets, force the fruit (especially citrus) through a juice extractor, peel and all, for greater flavour.*

STRAWBERRIES IN COGNAC

PERCHED HIGH on a cliff over Point Addis, Faye McLeish and Frank Lawrence have created a garden on rock. All the vegetables, herbs and flowers are growing in soil which has been carted from the settling ponds of the wool scouring works in Geelong. What natural soil they had on the ridge was cracked brickshot dispersed with slabs of ironstone. The scouring works composition was tested by the Department of Agriculture and consisted basically of composited sheep manure and sand.

No fertilisers or chemicals are used in the garden. Companion planting tomatoes and basil together and planting a few cabbages amongst the lettuce to attract the moths add special touches to a highly successful commercial garden. A favourite crop, broad beans, is planted early in autumn. A gap of 25 cm is left between each plant. The broad bean plant matures at between 4 and 5 months with a crop that continues for between 8 and 9 weeks.

Grosse Lisse and Burnley Surecrop tomatoes are planted around Melbourne Cup time in November. Maturing time takes 3½-4 months and the crop continues for about 12 weeks. Mixed lettuce is planted all year round. Seeds are blended with sand and sown over beds. Leaves are picked immature so that the lettuce keeps growing for many weeks. Strawberries grow in abundance all summer long.

2 punnets strawberries
3 teaspoons brown sugar
15 ml (3 teaspoons) Cognac

Using a wide bowl to serve, cut the strawberries into quarters with a sharp knife. Sprinkle with brown sugar and then the Cognac. Cover and leave overnight on the kitchen bench. Serve the next day with vanilla ice-cream.

Faye McLeish, Victoria

....

Strawberry leaf tea *(1840): 'Gather the leaves while young and tender, pick off the stalks, and dry in an airy but shady place. When sufficient quantity is collected, and they are perfectly dry, seal them in a bottle or canister and use as other tea leaves.'*

TAMARILLO JELLY

THE TAMARILLO belongs to the same family as the tomato. The fruit is botanically a many-seeded berry growing on an erect, shrubby, soft-wooded evergreen tree. The tree needs a rich, moist, well-drained soil. It is a shallow grower and heavy mulching is recommended.

8 red tamarillos
315 ml (1¼ cups) water
125 g (½ cup) sugar
10 g (3 teaspoons) gelatine
10 ml (2 teaspoons) muscat
   liqueur or port

Put the tamarillos in a bowl and cover with boiling water. Leave for 5 minutes and peel off the skins as they are very bitter. Chop the fruit into small pieces and put in a pan with the water and sugar. Simmer for 5 minutes. Remove from the heat and strain into a bowl without pressing the pulp through the sieve. The juice should be a clear red. Sprinkle the gelatine on top of the hot juice and stir until dissolved. Add the port or liqueur and pour into a glass bowl to set. Serve with pouring cream.

Lois Daish, New Zealand

RHUBARB AND STRAWBERRY CRUMBLE

500 g rhubarb
1 small punnet strawberries
10 g (1 tablespoon) flour
60 g (¼ cup) sugar

TOPPING
100 g flour
75 g butter
50 g brown sugar
60 g (½ cup) sliced almonds,
   roasted
1 teaspoon cinnamon
1 teaspoon lemon zest

Wash rhubarb well and cut into pieces. Hull the strawberries and mix with the rhubarb. Add the flour and sugar and toss together. Pile into a buttered gratin dish.

Make the topping by rubbing the butter into the flour and then stirring in the rest of the ingredients. Sprinkle over the fruit and bake at 180°C for about 45 minutes. Cover with loose foil if it starts to become too brown.

SERVES 4

Lois Daish, New Zealand

Fresh pineapple *is death to gelatine because it contains an enzyme called bromelain that breaks down the protein and setting quality. Canned pineapple can be used because it is cooked and the heating denatures the bromelain qualities.*

Quatre-épices *from France is used in French charcuterie. The proportions are variable, but basically it consists of 1 part ground cloves, to 3 parts ground ginger, to 4 parts ground nutmeg, to 12 parts ground pepper.*

Cakes, Biscuits & Breads

BLOW AWAY SPONGE

UNA GRAY writes:

'The freshness of the eggs is of the utmost importance in this recipe. If I can collect them from under the hen when I am about to bake, it will be a better cake. Failing this, it is important that the eggs be at room temperature. The cornflour is also of great importance; I use Nurse's brand, otherwise Fielders.'

¾ cup wheaten cornflour
1 heaped teaspoon plain flour
1 level teaspoon cream of tartar
½ level teaspoon bicarbonate of soda
4 eggs
pinch cooking salt
⅔ cup castor sugar

Place the flours, cream of tartar and bicarbonate of soda in a sieve and sift 3 times. Separate the eggs and place the whites in a stainless steel or glass bowl with the salt. Beat until light and fluffy; add the castor sugar while still beating. When the mixture is stiff and shiny, add the yolks one at a time and continue beating until thick enough to hold the figure '8' when dropped from the beaters. Gently fold in the sifted flours and divide between 2 well-greased and floured sponge pans. Bake at 190°C for 16 minutes. Turn out immediately onto kitchen paper that has been lightly dusted with castor sugar.

Una Gray, Queensland

To freeze *leftover egg yolk, place in a small container with a tiny pinch of salt for each yolk.*

BRAZIL HAZELNUT BREAD

5 egg whites at room
  temperature
pinch salt
170 g castor sugar
170 g plain flour
pinch cinnamon
155 g mixed brazil and
  hazelnuts

Beat the egg whites with the salt until stiff. Gradually add the sugar, beating well after each addition. Sift the flour and cinnamon and fold in a spoonful at a time. Fold in the nuts. Spoon the mixture into a lined and buttered loaf pan and bake for 35-45 minutes at 175°C. Cool in the tin. Wrap in foil and freeze. Slice into thin 'toasts' while frozen and bake at 150°C until golden around the edges.

Penny Smith, Victoria

BUTTERFLY CAKES

A MUST for fêtes and christenings!

2 cups self-raising flour
pinch salt
125 g butter
2/3 cup castor sugar
2 eggs
vanilla essence
6 tablespoons milk

Sift the flour and salt. Beat the butter and sugar in a bowl over hot water until light and fluffy. Beat the eggs and add them slowly with a few drops of vanilla essence. Beat in 2 tablespoons of the flour, then mix in the milk and flour alternately in small amounts, finishing with flour. Half fill patty pans with the mixture and bake in a fan-forced oven at 160°C for 15-20 minutes.

When cool, cut a hole in the top of the cakes with a spoon. Put whipped cream in each little hole, and then cut the cake tops in half and place them in the cream at an angle to make little wings. Dust with icing sugar and decorate with green jelly.

Marny Simpson, Victoria

To test *if an egg is fresh, hold it up to the light. If it is fresh, it will look clear.*

CHOCOLATE CAKE FROM GRANDMA APPS

I REMEMBER very little of my great-grandmother, but I can still picture her pantry and taste her chocolate cake. She lived somewhere in Elsternwick, in Melbourne, in a big old house. There were very large palms in the garden and a bunya pine we called a monkey tree because the branches used to drop and they looked like monkey tails lying on the ground. There was a croquet lawn too, but my clearest memory is of the green lino on the kitchen floor. Great-grandmother's kitchen had a particular smell—the polish, I suppose, as the floor shone like glass. There was a large walk-in pantry with tins on shelves far too high for me to investigate, and there was a conservatory with plants where we used to have tea.

Chocolate cake was the only treat I can remember and it was so good. She may well have made other cakes, but I know her moist, fudgy chocolate cake was my first conscious gastronomic experience. For years I forgot about that cake until one day, somewhere, something crossed my path and brought back to mind the smell of it in her kitchen. I could see the teapot with its knitted cosy and the jug with its doily of china beads. I rang Mum and the search was on. Where was the recipe for that cake? To my delight she found it, and very simple it is. The secret is to undercook it slightly so that the texture is moist and fudge-like. I wish we could tell my great-grandmother that a tiny bit of her cooking is still with us and appreciated.

juice of a lemon
1 cup milk
90 g soft butter
1 cup sugar
1 egg
2 tablespoons cocoa
1½ cups plain flour
½ teaspoon salt
1 teaspoon bicarbonate of
  soda

Strain the lemon juice into the milk and allow it to stand. Cream the butter and sugar until pale. Add the egg and beat until light, then fold in the curdled milk. Sift all the dry ingredients together and fold into the creamed butter mixture. Butter a 22 cm cake tin and pour in the batter. Bake at 175°C for about 30 minutes or until just cooked and slightly soft in the middle. Do not overcook or it will lose its fudgy texture.

ICING
30 g butter
1 tablespoon cream
1 tablespoon soft brown
  sugar
½ tablespoon cocoa
1½ -2 cups icing sugar,
  sifted

Melt the butter and cream in a pan with the brown sugar and cocoa, stirring to mix. Do not let it get too hot. Stir the butter mixture into the sifted icing sugar, adding a little boiling water if necessary. Cover the cake thickly with icing and allow to set before eating.

Penny Smith, Victoria

CHOCOLATE ÉCLAIRS

60 g butter
315 ml water
pinch salt
125 g plain flour
3 small eggs

Bring the butter, water and salt to the boil. Remove from the heat and stir in the flour until smooth. Cook gently until the mixture leaves the sides of the pan. Allow the mixture to become quite cold. Beat the eggs and add them gradually to the mixture, beating well after each addition. Using a 1 cm plain piping tube, pipe onto a greased tray in lengths of 7-9 cm. Bake at 230°C for about 30 minutes. Do not open the oven for the first 15 minutes of baking. When cooked, remove from the oven, pierce with a knife and cool. Fill with whipped cream and coat with chocolate icing.

CHOCOLATE ICING

1 dessertspoon cocoa
4 tablespoons water
knob of butter
1 teaspoon vanilla essence
250 g icing sugar

Cook the cocoa and water over a gentle heat until thickened. Add the butter. Allow to cool. When cold, add the vanilla essence and sufficient icing sugar to make a thick dropping consistency.

Marny Simpson, Victoria

....

To melt chocolate *successfully, break the pieces up and put in a small bowl. Stand the bowl in very hot water and stir from time to time. Excess heat, or any drop of moisture, will cause the chocolate to go grainy, burn and turn bitter.*

DAMPER

8 cups self-raising flour
2-2½ cups grated coconut
2-2½ teaspoons salt
3-4 eggs, depending on size
water

Using plenty of solid hardwood, or any wood that makes coals (black wattle is good), prepare the fire 2-2 ½ hours before you want to use it.

Mix the flour, coconut and salt thoroughly in a large bowl with a strong knife (this is reputed to keep the loaf light). Add the eggs and water very slowly until the dough is all joined together with no cracks and no dry mixture in the bottom. Dust with flour under and on top of the mixture to enable it to be lifted out of the bowl and placed in a camp oven which has been well-oiled, bottom and sides. Place the camp oven and the damper near the fire so as to warm them but not cook the dough. Leave for ½ to 1 hour before putting the dough on the camp fire to cook.

When the fire has nearly burnt out, scrape away most of the coals where the base of the oven is to sit, then put on 4 scoops of soil to stop the base from burning. Don't have any coals too close to the bottom of the oven. Place as many large, red-hot coals on top of the camp oven as possible and leave until the damper starts to smell cooked—usually about 45 minutes. Lift the lid and inspect to get the feel of how the top coals are cooking it. Once ready, the damper will keep hot in the oven for a long time. Serve with billy tea and cocky's joy (Golden Syrup).

SERVES 23

Max O'Brien, Far North Queensland

To tell if flour *is fresh, throw a small amount against a dry smooth surface. If it falls like powder, it is stale. Alternatively, squeeze a little in your hand and if it retains the shape given by your hand, it is good enough to use.*

DROP SCONES

125 g self-raising flour
pinch salt
1 level tablespoon castor
    sugar
1 egg
150 ml (7½ tablespoons)
    milk
lard for cooking

Sift the flour, salt and sugar into a bowl. Make a well in the centre and drop in the egg. Add the milk slowly, working in the flour until the mixture resembles a smooth batter. Strain the mixture into a jug. Heat a griddle pan to very hot with a small piece of lard. When a slight haze appears, pour on small amounts of batter, well separated. When the scones have puffed and bubbled on the surface, and are golden underneath, turn them over and brown the other side. Serve immediately with melted honey or real maple syrup and a dob of butter. If you are not eating them at once you may keep them within the folds of a clean tea-towel.

MAKES APPROX. 15

Marie Popperwell, England

GINGER FLUFF SPONGE

4 eggs
185 g (¾ cup) sugar
60 g (½ cup) arrowroot
2 dessertspoons plain flour
2 teaspoons ground ginger
2 teaspoons cinnamon
1 teaspoon cocoa
1 teaspoon cream of tartar
½ teaspoon bicarbonate of
    soda
1 dessertspoon golden syrup

FILLING
2 tablespoons butter
2 tablespoons sugar
2 tablespoons hot water
vanilla to taste
coconut

Beat the eggs until stiff. Add the sugar and continue to beat for 20 minutes. Sift the arrowroot, flour, ginger, cinnamon, cocoa, cream of tartar and bicarbonate of soda. Fold into the egg mixture and then add the golden syrup. Pour the batter into a buttered tin dusted with castor sugar and bake in a moderate oven for 15-20 minutes or until springy when touched. Cool on a wire rack.

Filling: Beat the butter, sugar, hot water and vanilla until thickened. Put between the two halves of the cake and on top. Sprinkle with coconut.

Miss L. F. Goodridge, Burra Burra Centenary
Cookery Book

FRUIT LOAF

THIS BREAD keeps very well and is also very good when made with 250 g fruit mince instead of the mixed fruits. The extra fat in the mince keeps the bread moist.

5 cups unbleached white
   bread flour
2 teaspoons salt
1 tablespoon dry yeast
2 teaspoons mixed spice
1 teaspoon cinnamon
1/2 teaspoon nutmeg
250 g mixed dried fruit—
   apricots, pears, peaches,
   sultanas, currants—
   chopped and soaked overnight in sherry or fruit juice
500 ml warm water
1 teaspoon honey
1 teaspoon oil
1/2 cup mixed peel (optional)
1/2 cup walnuts (optional)
1 egg, beaten
poppy seeds

Put all the dry ingredients and fruit in a large bowl and mix well. Using a sturdy wooden spoon, add the warm water, honey and oil. Turn the dough out onto a lightly floured surface and knead until smooth and elastic. Put the dough in a greased bowl, cover with a damp tea-towel and leave in a warm place to double in bulk. Punch down the dough and knead to smooth again (adding the mixed peel and walnuts if you are using them) before shaping into small loaves and placing in well-greased bread tins or free-form cobs onto a greased baking tray. Glaze with a beaten egg and top with poppy seeds. Bake for 30 minutes at 230°C, checking to see it does not over-brown.

Joan Joyce, Victoria

DELICATE, DELICIOUS CHEESE BISCUITS

75 g plain flour
50 g butter, cubed
75 g mature cheddar, grated
1/2 teaspoon salt
pinch dry mustard
pinch cayenne
1 egg yolk
1/2 teaspoon lemon juice

Put the flour and butter into a food processor and mix until it resembles coarse breadcrumbs. Add the cheese, salt, mustard and cayenne. Process until just combined. Beat the egg yolk with the lemon juice, add to the flour and process until the mixture 'balls'. Iced water may be added to make it soft but not sticky. Pat the dough into a cushion shape and refrigerate for 30 minutes. Preheat oven to 200°C. Roll out as thinly as possible and cut into shapes. Bake for 5 minutes or until a pale golden colour.

Lizzie Marshall, Far North Queensland

LEMON POUND CAKE WITH GIN SYRUP

1 lemon
200 g castor sugar
250 g butter
5 eggs
250 g flour
1 teaspoon baking powder
100 g candied peel, chopped

SYRUP
juice of 2 lemons
150 g castor sugar
40 ml (2 tablespoons) gin

Preheat oven to 180°C. Grate zest from lemon and add to the sugar and soft butter in a bowl (you can use a food processor). Cream the mixture until pale. Add the eggs one at a time, beating well between each addition. Squeeze the lemon and add the juice. Sift the flour and baking powder together and stir into the creamed base with the candied peel. Spoon the mixture into a buttered, floured, round 22 cm cake tin and bake for 35 minutes or until the cake is springy when touched.

While the cake is baking, mix the syrup ingredients together. When the cake is cooked turn it out, right side up, into a dish with sides. Prick the top with a fork and pour the syrup over the hot cake. As it cools the topping will form a light sugary crust.

Lois Daish, New Zealand

MELTING MOMENTS

125 g butter
30 g icing sugar
60 g plain flour
60 g cornflour

Cream the butter and sugar, then add the flour and cornflour. Roll out into small balls and place them on a baking sheet, pressing down with a fork to flatten a little and make indentations. Bake in a moderate oven (175°C) for about 15 minutes until the colour of pale straw.

Penny Smith, Victoria

To save time *when making a pastry case, follow the desired recipe, roll out and line the selected tin, prick the base thoroughly and freeze, instead of rolling the pastry into a ball and resting in the refrigerator. Preheat the oven to 200°C, bake the shell for 5-8 minutes and turn the heat down to 175°C until golden brown. Cool before filling.*

MERINGUES

Equal amounts egg whites, granulated sugar and castor sugar

Spray several baking sheets with a non-stick spray. Weigh the egg whites. Weigh the same amount of granulated and castor sugars separately. Beat the egg whites until absolutely stiff. Beat in the granulated sugar. Fold in the castor sugar, a spoonful at a time. Spoon the mixture into a forcing bag. Pipe onto the baking sheets in the desired shape and bake at 80°C until they come off the tray easily. Leave to rest in the oven overnight.

Penny Smith, Victoria

NUT CARAMEL TARTS

MILLIE MAKES these delicious tarts in small, boat-shaped tartlet tins.

PASTRY
125 g unsalted butter
125 g castor sugar
1 egg
250 g flour
1/2 teaspoon baking powder

FILLING
1/2 cup sugar
1/2 cup cream, scalded
250 g slivered toasted almonds

Pastry: Cream the butter and sugar, add the egg, then the flour and baking powder. Form the pastry into a ball and cut it into four. Stack the pieces on top of each other and flatten. Repeat this twice more. Roll out and cut into circles to fit your tartlet tins (use any size you wish). Prick the pastry bases thoroughly and bake in a moderate oven at 190°C for 10-12 minutes or until nicely browned. Cool.
Filling: Make a caramel with the sugar by cooking it in a heavy pan until it browns. Add the hot cream and stir to melt the caramel. Remove from the heat and toss in the almonds. Spoon the praline into the cooled pastry shells and return to the oven at 180°C for 5 minutes. Cool completely and store in a tightly sealed jar.

Millie Sherman, New South Wales

OLD-FASHIONED APPLE CAKE

GAI ADCOCK writes:

Around the turn of the century, Peter Sutherland had a stud cattle farm at Thologolong on the Upper Murray River. Here he bred some of the finest Aberdeen Angus cattle you could ever wish to see. His beautiful black bulls were all imported from Britain and he was justifiably proud of them.

During the drought in 1902-3 many of his cows died and he was forced to ask his neighbours for help. He was sold fifty head and he began to rebuild his herd. One of the cows in the lot was a light roan colour. She didn't appeal to him and he put her in a different paddock that was next to his precious Angus bulls. Nature took its course and twelve months later this particular cow dropped her first calf. It was described as 'mulberry' in colour. Peter was not impressed but his wife Eva was, and she kept the cow and calf. For twelve successive years the cow duly dropped a calf and Eva managed to keep them all from the butcher.

In the mid-1930s Peter died and the property was sold. So popular had the unusually coloured cows become that his daughter-in-law Helen couldn't bear to part with them, and she bought them. With eight cows and four bulls and Eva's help, she systematically selected and cross-bred what she referred to as her 'Murray Greys'. The now world-renowned Murray Grey breed grew from there.

When Brenton and I bought our property in the Adelaide Hills eighteen years ago we had a commercial apple orchard as well as a mixed herd, including three Murray Grey cows. I loved their soft silvery colour. They were such docile beasts and so easy to handle. They were also very good at rearing their young. Their progeny sold for more than those of the other cattle so we decided to concentrate on breeding Murray Greys ourselves. From those three cows the Amorilla Murray Grey Stud was born.

185 g butter
250 g self-raising flour
60 g cornflour
1 large or 2 small egg yolks
1 teaspoon vanilla
milk or water
185 g sugar
1 kg Granny Smith apples stewed in very little water, drained overnight and then puréed

Rub the butter into the sifted flours. Mix enough milk or water with the egg yolk and vanilla to make ⅔ cup. Add with the sugar to the flour mixture (it will be quite sticky). Chill for 30 minutes in the refrigerator. Butter two 18 cm sponge cake tins and line them with baking paper. Cut the pastry into two equal portions. Cut each portion into two again and, with floured hands, gently roll the dough then press into the bottom of each tin. Spoon in an even layer of apple purée and cover with the remaining pastry. Bake at 225°C for 20 minutes. When cool, ice with lemon icing, and sprinkle with nutmeg.

Gai Adcock, South Australia

OLIVE BREAD

1¹/₄ cups warm water
¹/₂ teaspoon sugar
1¹/₂ tablespoons Fermipan
*   yeast*
375 g baker's flour
¹/₂ teaspoon salt
2 tablespoons virgin olive
*   oil*
¹/₄ cup chopped black olives
2 tablespoons olive paste
3 or 4 sun-dried tomatoes

Combine the warm water, sugar and yeast in a plastic jug and leave in a warm spot to prove. Put the flour and salt into a bowl and add the oil and the yeast mixture, which should by now be frothing. Stir with a round-bladed knife until all the liquid is absorbed. Turn the dough mass onto a table top and knead for 5-10 minutes or until smooth and satiny in texture. Oil the bowl and replace the dough, cover with plastic wrap and set in a warm place to double in bulk. Knead the dough once more, adding the olives and paste, and roll out to fit a Swiss roll tin. Oil the tin well and press the dough into it. Cut the sun-dried tomatoes into slivers and press into the surface of the dough. Allow the dough to rise to twice its size again and then bake at 210°C for 7 minutes until the bread sounds hollow when tapped. Cool on a rack. Wonderful served with pâté.

Tricia Hennessy, Victoria

Eggs and sugar *beat to a creamy smoothness if they are slightly warmed. Your cake will be lighter if you warm the mixing bowl and sugar, or warm the eggs and sugar in the microwave for 6 seconds, before beating.*

POND COTTAGE ALMOND CAKE

125 g butter
100 g almond meal
3 egg whites
150 g castor sugar
1 teaspoon vanilla essence
50 g plain flour
30 g extra butter
1 cup blanched almonds
1 tablespoon honey

Put the butter into a saucepan to melt. Cool. Add the almond meal, egg whites and sugar and stir together with a wooden spoon. Then add the vanilla essence and flour and mix thoroughly. Line a 20 cm cake tin with a removable base and spoon in the mixture. Bake at 175°C for 15 minutes or until almost done.

Meanwhile, put the butter in a small saucepan with the almonds and honey. Stir over heat until well mixed. Remove the almost-cooked cake from the oven and coat with the almond and honey mixture. Put the cake back into the oven to set for about 5 minutes until the almonds are golden and the honey has coated them with a toffee glaze.

Nellie Ramsay, Victoria

PRUE'S SPONGE CAKE WITH FRESH EGGS

PRUE HAS her own chooks and an abundant supply of fresh eggs. She makes sponges to sell in local restaurants in her spare time. She now has emus—one wonders what kind of cakes she will create next!

6 eggs, separated
3/4 cup castor sugar
3/4 cup cornflour
1 tablespoon custard powder
1/2 teaspoon bicarbonate of
  soda
1 teaspoon cream of tartar

Beat the egg whites until stiff peaks form. While beating, gradually add the sugar and continue to beat until the sugar has dissolved. Add the egg yolks and beat for a further 2 minutes or until creamy. Sift the dry ingredients together and carefully fold into the beaten meringue. Pour the mixture into a greased 26 cm springform tin lined with baking paper and cook in a moderate oven (175°C) for 25 minutes or until the cake feels springy when touched. Turn out onto a wire rack covered with a clean tea-towel. Allow to sit for 1 or 2 minutes then move to another cake rack to cool. This makes one layer of my giant sponge.

Prue Rosser, Victoria

PRUE'S FRUIT CAKE

PRUE AND I made this fruit cake together for my daughter's wedding and it was perfect.

1¼ kg mixed fruit,
  including cherries,
  sultanas, currants, raisins
  and apricots
6 tablespoons brandy
250 g butter
1⅓ cups soft brown sugar
1 teaspoon almond essence
2 tablespoons golden syrup
12 eggs
60 g almonds
2 cups plain flour
30 g cornflour
2 teaspoons mixed spice
½ teaspoon bicarbonate of
  soda
1 teaspoon ground nutmeg

Line a 20 cm tin with 2 layers of brown paper. Steep the fruit in the brandy overnight. Cream the butter and sugar, almond essence and golden syrup together until light. Add the eggs separately, beating well after each addition. Stir in the fruit, the almonds and the sifted dry ingredients. Mix carefully and spoon into the prepared cake tin. Tap the tin on the bench to dispel any air bubbles and cook for 3½ hours in a slow (150°C) oven. Brush with a little brandy and leave to cool in the tin. Brush with brandy again from time to time before you ice the cake and keep in an airtight container.

To make bigger cakes (as for layered cakes): 1½ times the quantity will fill a 23 cm cake tin and take 5-5½ hours to cook. Twice the quantity will fit a 25 cm tin and take 6-6½ hours to cook.

Prue Rosser, Victoria

Brandy sprinkled *over fruit cake when it comes out of the oven will give it a far richer flavour.*

SAFFRON BRIOCHE

575 g plain flour
1 level tablespoon Fermipan
    yeast
2 level tablespoons castor
    sugar
1/2 level teaspoon salt
1/4 teaspoon powdered
    saffron
4 large eggs
120 ml warmed milk
100 g softened butter
1 egg yolk, mixed with a
    little water, for the glaze

Sift the flour into a bowl. Add the rest of the dry ingredients. Beat the eggs with the milk. Make a well in the centre of the flour and, using a wooden spoon or an electric mixer with a dough hook, work in the egg/milk liquid thoroughly to form a very soft dough. Add the butter, mix well and cover the bowl with plastic wrap. Leave in a warm place to double in bulk. Punch the dough down and knead with your hands for 5 minutes, flouring them if you need to. Cover the bowl and refrigerate again overnight.

The next day, butter the tin or moulds. Knead the chilled dough until completely smooth. Divide equally into small balls for small moulds or put the dough into the prepared bread tin. Brush with glaze, cover, and leave to rise in a warm place. Preheat the oven to 200°C and bake the brioche for about 15 minutes until pale golden. Cool on a rack.

Penny Smith, Victoria

Line biscuit tins *with a circle of blotting paper before sealing to help keep the biscuits crisp.*

SHORTBREAD BISCUITS

SHORTBREAD BISCUITS have always been irresistible. During my first trip to Canada, Isobel Cooper baked several batches and packed them into a tin to travel with us to the Rockies. She used to send them down to me in Australia by mail, and I was always delighted to receive them. Try as I have, I cannot quite get the texture Isobel achieved. Here is her delicious recipe.

315 g soft butter
vanilla
1 cup icing sugar
½ cup cornflour
2½ cups flour
pinch salt

Cream the butter and vanilla in an electric mixer. Sift all the dry ingredients together and add them slowly, spoonful by spoonful, while the mixer is on slow and making sure each addition is incorporated before adding the next. Preheat the oven to 160°C. Lightly roll teaspoonfuls of dough and put them on baking trays. Press each one with a fork and put the trays into the oven. Turn down the heat to 150°C and cook for 15 minutes. They should not colour. Cool completely on a wire rack. Seal in an airtight tin and the biscuits will last any journey around the world.

Isobel Cooper, Canada

WALNUT AND FIG CAKE

185 g self-raising flour
1 level teaspoon bicarbonate
    of soda
1 teaspoon allspice
pinch salt
60 g butter
185 g sugar
2 eggs
185 g dried figs, chopped
2 tablespoons brandy
185 g walnuts, chopped

Butter two 25 cm cake tins. Sift the flour, bicarbonate of soda, allspice and salt. Cream the butter and sugar, add the eggs and beat until fluffy. Warm the figs in the brandy and allow to plump and become soft. Add the sifted ingredients to the butter and sugar mixture and fold in the figs and walnuts. Spoon into the tins and bake in a preheated oven at 175°C for 30-40 minutes.

Penny Smith, Victoria

SPONGE CAKE WITH PINK AND WHITE ICING

TWO-EGG SPONGE

*(bake in a 20 cm round cake
    tin for 20 minutes)*
2 eggs
2 tablespoons cornflour
2 tablespoons plain flour
*2 tablespoons self-raising
    flour*
⅓ cup castor sugar

THREE-EGG SPONGE

*(bake in two deep 17 cm round
    cake tins for 15 minutes or
    in a 25 cm x 30 cm Swiss roll
    pan for 12 minutes)*
3 eggs
¼ cup cornflour
¼ cup plain flour
¼ cup self-raising flour
½ cup castor sugar

FOUR-EGG SPONGE

*(bake in two deep 20 cm round
    cake tins for 20 minutes or
    one deep 23 cm round cake
    tin for 40 minutes)*
4 eggs
⅓ cup cornflour
⅓ cup plain flour
⅓ cup self-raising flour
⅔ cup castor sugar

Have the eggs at room temperature. Grease the tins. Sift the flours 3 times. Beat the eggs until smooth and creamy (this is best done in the small bowl of an electric mixer for about 7 minutes). Add the sugar a tablespoon at a time. When the sugar is dissolved, put the mixture into a larger basin and fold in the sifted flours very gently with a spatula. Spread the mixture evenly into the cake tin or tins and bake in a moderate oven. The sponge will shrink from the side of the tin when cooked and the top will feel springy when touched. Cool on a wire rack. Ice with pink and white icing.

Marney Simpson, Victoria

To make *self-raising flour, combine 2 kg plain flour, 60 g
cream of tartar and 30 g bicarbonate of soda, and sift 3 times.*

CAMPING AND GAIL'S MUESLI

CAMPING IN the Australian bush can be quite a challenge for the inventive epicurean. I have often stayed in my tent contemplating breakfast with anticipation, feeling inordinately hungry and hoping someone would get the fire going to prepare the coals needed to cook on.

Waking to the multi-musical calls of a lyrebird is an experience I could get used to. With the sun barely showing its face above the horizon, these lovely birds scratch around the leaf mulch surrounding my tent unaware that only a thin sheet of canvas separates us, or perhaps not caring as they rejoice in the dawn of a new day in the forest.

I lie there, chilled, it's true, for the Gippsland rainforest in April can be wet and cold, but I begin to sense my surroundings even before I am fully conscious. The sound of wood-chopping is encouraging—fire and warmth, hot water to follow, a pannikin of steaming tea, and water to wash the sleep from my eyes. The ground is cold, moist and soft as I tread, my naked feet feeling deliciously cushioned by the leaves that have fallen from the towering giants overhead which spread their protective canopy above the forest floor. I am hungry—horse-eating hungry—and I dress quickly to make my way to the fire.

Breakfast in the bush is a special experience. Why do I enjoy food there that I would never eat at home? I eat rashers of bacon crisped on an open fire until the salt stings the tongue, eggs—not one, but two—flecked with ash, and toast, burnt around the edges, moist with butter and coated with jam, as I gaze at the wonderland before me and take in the peace and presence of the centuries-old forum. I am content beyond measure.

The spit and crackle of the wood, the waft of vaporous smoke streaming slowly in the stillness, shafts of light through the leaves—all collaborate to prepare the soul and replenish the body. A perfect new day, and I have it all before me to walk as I please through the forest and along the coast of East Gippsland. In the early morning the dingo has already trod, collecting the half-eaten fish tossed aside by another predator during the night. The pied oyster-catchers are already at work on the rocks and the muttonbirds in their thousands have begun their migration this April day across the waves to warmer lands. How beautiful this day—this gift of light and colour, texture and time. Croajingolong National Park is a treasure Australia has inherited for even the most humble to enjoy.

Gail's muesli mixture is ideal for camping trips. Prepare it at home and take in a sealed jar. A bowl of this before starting out on your day's activities will not only taste good, it will be good for you and sustain you until lunchtime. I had this at Meryl Bowers' celebratory breakfast party at The Hermitage in Great Western, Victoria, on Australia Day morning. Friends from around the area contributed their special breakfast recipes. ▶

¹/₂ cup honey
¹/₂ cup salad oil
750 g rolled oats
2 cups wheatgerm
1 cup coconut
¹/₂ cup sesame seeds
1 teaspoon ground
  cinnamon
¹/₂ cup bran flakes
chopped dried fruit
sultanas
chopped nuts (such as flaked
  almonds, brazil nuts and
  hazelnuts)
pumpkin kernels
sunflower seeds

Warm the honey and oil and mix through the oats, wheatgerm, coconut, sesame seeds, cinnamon and bran flakes. Bake in a moderate oven for half an hour, stirring every 10 minutes. When cold, add the rest of the ingredients. Keep in a well sealed jar.

Gail Freeman, New Zealand

When baking bread, *use the water in which you have boiled potatoes for added nourishment and flavour.*

◇ ◇ ◇ NOTES ◇ ◇ ◇

Nutmeg and mace *are from the same tree. Mace is the outer lacy casing surrounding the hard, brown nutmeg seed. When peeled away it is dried to become mace, which is more subtle in flavour. It takes 5 kg of nutmeg to produce 2 kg of mace.*

Jams, Preserves Pickles & Chutneys

BLACKBERRY AND CRAB-APPLE JELLY

blackberries and crab-apples
in equal quantities
water
sugar

Chop whole crab-apples into small pieces. Add equal quantities of blackberries to the pot and just cover with water. Bring slowly to the boil and simmer for 1 hour. Strain the mixture through a jelly bag.

For each 625 ml (2½ cups) of liquid add 500 g sugar. Stir over heat to dissolve sugar. Bring to the boil and boil for 30-45 minutes. Test for setting by dipping spoon in jelly—it is done when 2 drops join before falling from the spoon. Bottle and seal.

Annie Thomas, South Australia

CHRISTMAS PEACHES TO SERVE WITH HAM

1500 ml apple cider vinegar
1 cup sugar
3 sticks cinnamon
8 white peppercorns
6 whole cloves
4 star anise
3-4 pieces dried orange peel
16 firm but ripe yellow
peaches
½ cup Peach liqueur
a 2-litre jar with a rubber
sealed stopper

Put the vinegar, sugar, spices and orange peel into a heavy pot. Bring to the boil, stirring to dissolve the sugar. Carefully immerse the peaches into the hot liquid and allow to poach gently until just cooked (about 3-5 minutes). Test with a fine needle. They must remain firm and hold their shape.

Remove the fruit with a slotted spoon and allow it to cool. Peel carefully and arrange in layers in the jar. Reduce the poaching liquid by about half and turn off the heat. When cool, add the peach liqueur. Pour this over the peaches, making sure the fruit is covered with syrup, and seal the jar. Leave for at least 3 weeks before using.

Penny Smith, Victoria

To prevent jam *from going mouldy and in the absence of wax, cut rounds of tissue paper the size of the jars and soak them separately in vinegar. Lay them close over the top of the jam and seal in the normal way.*

FEIJOA PASTE

THE FEIJOA or pineapple guava is a decorative shrub or small tree that bears abundant fruit in autumn. It dictates its own timetable; the fruit falls when ripe and is collected from under the shrub. It should not be picked. The fruit can be used in chutneys and jams, or combined with other autumn fruit such as crab-apples, grapes, pomegranates, persimmons, tamarillos, passionfruit and spices to make a delicious dessert jelly. It is highly perfumed with a strong exotic flavour. The sharpness of lemon helps offset a somewhat cloying sweetness.

Feijoa paste is made in a similar way to the more familiar quince paste. The basic ingredients of a fruit paste or cheese are equal weights of fruit purée and sugar, but you can adjust the proportions slightly according to taste. A little butter will prevent a scum from forming.

Halve the feijoa and scoop out the flesh with a teaspoon. Simmer in a large shallow saucepan until melted and then mash or put through a mouli. Measure and add an equal weight of white sugar, and the juice and rind of a lemon for each kilo of fruit—more or less as desired. Using a wooden spoon, stir over gentle heat until the mixture is thick. It is done when the mixture comes away from the sides and you can see the bottom of the saucepan when you stir. This can take up to an hour. Continuous stirring is necessary to prevent sticking, so you may need to call for reinforcements. As the mixture will begin to splutter and plop like a geyser towards the end, wear oven gloves for protection.

When done, pour the mixture into a lightly oiled shallow rectangular dish or into a series of small sterilised glass jars or porcelain moulds. They should be straight-sided so the paste can be turned out. Seal the small containers and store in a dark cool place for at least 3 months. The large mould can be turned out after several days and the fruit paste cut into blocks, wrapped in plastic film and kept in the refrigerator for up to 12 months. It can also be frozen.

To serve, turn out the fruit paste onto a board or plate where it can be sliced like a cheese. It makes a delicious addition to a cheese platter, going particularly well with soft cheeses such as brie, chèvre and creamy blue.

Trish Ridley, Victoria

Seal jams, *chutneys and pickles that you intend to store with melted paraffin wax.*

DRIED APRICOT, PINEAPPLE AND GINGER JAM

400 g dried apricots
4 circles dried pineapple
3 litres boiling water
2 kg sugar
10 pieces crystallised ginger
½ cup kirsch or white rum

Chop the apricot and pineapple into small pieces and put into a preserving pan. Cover with the water and allow to stand overnight. Bring the mixture to the boil and continue to cook until the liquid is reduced by two thirds. Stir in the sugar and keep stirring until it has dissolved. Continue to cook without stirring until the mixture sets on a cold saucer forming a skin.

Slice the ginger finely and add to the jam off the heat with the liqueur. Bottle into sterile jars and seal.

Penny Smith, Victoria

FRESH GOOSEBERRY CHUTNEY

225 g freshly picked
    gooseberries
2 tablespoons coriander
    leaves, stalks and roots,
    chopped
1 red chilli
1 shallot
½ teaspoon cumin powder
pinch salt
pinch sugar
pinch chilli powder
10 ml (2 teaspoons) fresh
    ginger juice
water

Wash the gooseberries and trim off the stalks. Cut the gooseberries in half. Put them into a blender with the coriander, chilli, shallot, spices and seasonings. Add the ginger juice and process to a coarse texture. Add a little water to make the mixture a chutney consistency and chill before serving.

This chutney is delicious with cold meats or meats that have been marinated with eastern spices.

Betty Bray, New South Wales

To candy dill pickles *for an interesting variation, drain them from their original brine and pack them into jars. Pour on a heavy sugar syrup and allow to stand sealed for a month before using.*

GOOSEBERRY JELLY

GOOSEBERRIES (*Ribes grossularia*) grow best in cool, moist conditions. Because the fruit ripens early it is often damaged by frost and will split in the wet. The plants need protection from strong winds and hot sunshine.

Before planting, prepare the beds with animal manure, superphosphate and potassium sulphate. The soil must be well-drained, but gooseberries will tolerate a wider range of soil than most other berries. Mulching and watering during growth is essential, as they do not like to dry out. Successful propagation can be achieved from one-year-old hardwood cuttings with at least five buds.

On planting, leave no more than four shoots and prune back to 30 cm to an outside bud. The bush should start bearing when three years old. In the first two years it is important to develop a good framework of vigorous shoots with an open centre. Prune back all shoots to a third, removing any suckers and weak shoots from the base. At five years of age all shoots should be removed as they produce poor-quality fruit.

When green the fruit is excellent for pies and jellies. As it ripens the fruit is delicious eaten fresh.

1.75 kg gooseberries, washed
1.75 litres (7 cups) water
several sprigs basil in a
*   muslin bag (optional)*
sugar

Put the gooseberries in a pan with the water and the basil. Bring to the boil and reduce the heat. Simmer for 45 minutes until the fruit is completely soft. Strain through a jelly bag. Measure the juice and add 500 g sugar for every 625 ml of juice. Stir the mixture over low heat until the sugar has dissolved, then boil rapidly for about 10 minutes or until setting point is reached. Remove the basil and then put in bottles.

Betty Bray, New South Wales

QUICK REDCURRANT JELLY

125 g jar pure redcurrant
*   jelly*
2 tablespoons port
2 tablespoons fresh
*   redcurrants*

Melt the jelly in a pan with the port and whisk over a gentle heat until smooth. Throw in the redcurrants and heat through just before serving.

Penny Smith, Victoria

QUINCE CHEESE

AUTUMN with its magic colours and heady smells is the end of the tomato season and a time for making chutney and sauce to store through the long winter months. The ancient quince, that has corrupted the senses since biblical times, comes into its own. Its downy skin and golden tints turn to ruby rust when cooked slowly, and the house is filled with its aroma. 'Cheese', made by simmering quinces for hours over gentle heat, stores well to complement the tart and grainy texture of a good cheddar. To give a deliciously scented flavour to an apple pie, add 2 tablespoons of quince purée to the sliced or cooked apples.

1½ kg freshly picked quinces
300 ml pure apple juice
1 whole lemon, quartered
1¼ kg white sugar

Rub the fur from the quince skin. Chop the fruit roughly, including the core and skin, and place in a large preserving pan. Add the apple juice and lemon. Simmer, covered, for 30 minutes. Remove the lid and continue to cook to a pulp. Pass the fruit and lemon through a mouli and return it to the pan. The mixture should not be sloppy wet. Add the sugar and stir until dissolved. Barely simmer this gooey mess for 4-5 hours, stirring every now and then to prevent sticking. It will thicken and change to a beautiful russet colour.

Spread the purée onto a non-stick baking tray about 2.5 cm thick and put it in a convection oven on the lowest setting for another 3-4 hours. Cut the mixture into squares and put back into the oven to dry out the cut sides. Store in airtight containers in the refrigerator.

Penny Smith, Victoria

RAISINS IN TOKAY

PLACE BUNCHES of dried raisins in a large glass jar with a small piece of cinnamon bark and a piece of dried orange skin. Cover with liqueur tokay. Let stand for at least a week. Drain and serve with a good brie, cheddar or creamy blue cheese on a platter. Seeded raisins may be used if preferred.

Raisins thus prepared will keep almost indefinitely. When you've finished draining the raisins, drink the liqueur!

David Hay, South Australia

SPICED ORANGES

6 whole oranges
500 g castor sugar
125 ml water
8 whole cloves
2 bay leaves
piece of blade mace
½ cinnamon stick
2 tablespoons brandy
2 tablespoons Grand
    Marnier
cream
6 sprigs fresh mint
pistachio nuts

Zest the oranges using the finest grater. Put the zest aside and remove the pith from the oranges. Select a heavy-based pan and put the sugar into it over a gentle heat. When the sugar begins to melt and caramelise it will emit brown bubbles around the sides. Pour in the water (it will spit, so take care). Using gloves, pick up the pan and rotate it until the sugar and water combine to make a syrup. Add the cloves, bay leaves, mace, cinnamon and orange zest. Allow to simmer for a few minutes and add the whole oranges. Turn them in the syrup for 5 minutes. Cool, then chill.

When ready to serve, remove the oranges with a slotted spoon and slice them into thin rounds. Strain the syrup and add the liqueurs. Pour the syrup over the sliced oranges and serve with cream, mint and pistachio nuts. The oranges can be prepared days in advance, sealed and refrigerated.

SERVES 6

Penny Smith, Victoria

LEMON BUTTER

TRICIA HENNESSY writes:
Herewith my Nana's lemon butter recipe, one of the delights of my childhood. It is wonderful on scones.

250 g butter
250 g castor sugar
juice of 4 medium lemons
4 eggs

Soften the butter, and beat well with the sugar and lemon juice. Add the beaten eggs. In a double boiler over a gentle heat stir constantly until thickened. Cool, set into jars and seal.

Tricia Hennessy, Victoria

TOMATO CHUTNEY

1 kg freshly picked ripe
   tomatoes, chopped
1 small chilli, finely chopped
1 onion, chopped
2 cloves garlic, crushed
5 cm piece fresh ginger,
   minced
2 tablespoons sultanas
350 g brown sugar
1 tablespoon salt
1 teaspoon pepper
3 level teaspoons dry
   mustard powder
1 teaspoon allspice
340 ml cider vinegar

Put all the ingredients into a preserving pan and simmer for an hour or until thickened, stirring regularly. Bottle while still hot. Seal with a little olive oil and an airtight lid.

Penny Smith, Victoria

To make fruit jellies (*e.g. quince, redcurrant, etc.*), *put the fruit in a pan, cover with water, add 1 tablespoon lemon pips tied in a muslin bag, and boil for 20 minutes. Strain the juice through muslin without pressing on the fruit pulp and measure. Add 500 g sugar to each pint of liquid. Boil until set.*

RUBY NEIL'S CHUTNEYS AND RELISHES

HOWARD NEIL is a friend and enthusiastic cook who shares his talents with me from time to time. One of the few times I persuaded him to cook for me he made some delicious chutneys to accompany a beautiful eastern-style meal. The recipes came from his mother's cookbook. Written by hand, the book is full of recipes collected in New Zealand in the early 1940s. Ruby Neil lived in the tiny town of Paeroera. Whenever friends gathered for social occasions they swapped recipes, and her little book is full of recipes she enjoyed from her friends.

PEAR CHUTNEY

1.4 kg firm pears, peeled,
cored and roughly
chopped
400 g white sugar
800 ml malt vinegar
400 g sultanas
500 g dates, pitted but left
whole
2 tablespoons salt
1 teaspoon minced garlic
1 tablespoon cayenne

Put all the ingredients into a large pan and simmer for 3 hours, stirring occasionally. Bottle and seal. Makes enough for four 600 ml jars.

TOMATO RELISH

3 kg tomatoes, cored and cut
into wedges
1 kg onions, cut into rings
700 g white sugar
1 tablespoon curry powder
50 g salt
2 tablespoons dry mustard
1 tablespoon mixed spice
malt vinegar
2 tablespoons flour

Put the tomatoes, onions, sugar, curry powder, salt, mustard and mixed spice into a large saucepan. Pour in enough vinegar to almost cover. Boil for an hour. Mix the flour with a little extra vinegar and add to the relish. Simmer until thickened. Bottle and seal. Makes enough for four 600 ml jars.

INDIAN PICKLE

2 kg green apples, peeled,
  cored and finely sliced
200 g salt
50 g raisins
1 kg sultanas
100 g preserved ginger
1 teaspoon minced chilli
2 teaspoons dry mustard
1.2 litres malt vinegar
2 kg brown sugar

Prepare the apples and put them in a dish with the salt, raisins, sultanas, ginger, chilli, mustard and half the vinegar and let stand overnight. Boil the remaining vinegar with the sugar until it becomes a thick syrup. Remove from the heat. When cold, add the apple mixture. Bottle and seal. Best after 6 weeks' storage in a warm place. Makes enough for eight 600 ml jars.

TAMARILLO CHUTNEY

IT IS necessary to remove the skin from the tamarillos first because of its very bitter flavour—even possums won't eat it! Blanch the tamarillos in boiling water and they will peel easily.

1 kg tamarillos, skinned and
  cut in half
300 g green apples, peeled,
  cored and diced
400 g onions, roughly
  chopped
1¹/₂ teaspoons salt
¹/₂ teaspoon cayenne
120 g raisins
400 g brown sugar
300 ml malt vinegar
¹/₂ teaspoon ground allspice
¹/₄ teaspoon cracked black
  pepper
¹/₄ teaspoon ground cloves
1 teaspoon minced chilli

Combine the skinned tamarillos and the remaining ingredients in a large saucepan. Simmer gently for 1-1¹/₂ hours until thick. Pour into hot jars and seal. Makes enough for four 400 ml jars.

Ruby Neil, New Zealand

....

Do not boil jams *on a high heat. It may cook them faster but it destroys their bright colour.*

Seal pickles *when cold with hot paraffin wax
and the vinegar will not evaporate.*

◇ ◇ ◇ NOTES ◇ ◇ ◇

Allow jam *made from berries to cool before spooning into jars—the fruit will not sink to the bottom.*

Cheese

THE BASIC PRINCIPLES OF CHEESEMAKING

IN AUSTRALIA, the milk is pasteurised, then bacterial culture is added causing it to curdle. A separating agent is added to help divide the solids from the whey. This separating agent can be animal or vegetable rennet, or lactic acid in the case of fresh cheeses. The curds are then cut, fully drained, put into moulds and left to ripen. Following this basic procedure the process unfolds in different ways for different cheeses.

Cheeses derive their distinctive character firstly from the type of milk from which they are made. Further variations occur from the earliest stages of cheese production. To start with, the curds may be scalded or cooked to different temperatures. This process, and how the curds are cut, broadly determines the texture of the finished cheese. Thirdly, it is in the moulding, preserving and finishing phases that the strongest changes in texture, taste and appearance can take place. Once moulded, the cheese may be soaked in brine, waxed, exposed to bacteria, rinsed with water or alcohol, smoked, covered with herbs or simply left to ripen. During the ripening the temperature and humidity conditions in storage are carefully monitored to produce different effects (e.g. blue vein in blue cheese, white floury rind on camembert, holes in Swiss cheese, etc.).

There are three main varieties of cheese, namely fresh, soft and hard cheeses, and eight sub-categories: fresh cheeses, soft unpressed cheeses, medium rind soft cheeses, blue cheeses, goat and sheep's milk cheeses, pressed hard and semi-hard cheeses and cooked hard cheeses.

When Buying and Storing Cheese

- Find a cheese retailer who knows what he or she is doing and whom you can trust to guide you in what is best for your requirements.

- Never buy too much in advance. Try and buy for one or two meals only. If in doubt, taste the product prior to buying.

- Select according to the nature of the cheese, the time it takes to ripen, the best milk. Modern dairy technology has greatly reduced the likelihood of cheeses developing faults, particularly the more commercial varieties available in Australia. However, different chemical and biological conditions do alter the nature of the end product, particularly in farmhouse products. Remember the seasonal lactation (cows, sheep and goats) and that generally speaking, spring, mid-summer and autumn are the prime months for cheesemaking.

- Most cheeses can be wrapped in plastic wrap or foil to avoid moisture loss. With surface-ripened cheese, this rule applies unless the cheese is whole, such as camembert, when the cheese should be left in its original wrapper. It is important to understand how a camembert or brie ripens (from the rind inwards, taking from one month to 45 days) and to be patient with this natural process.

- You can always check on the stage of the cheese by cutting a wedge. If it is not ready, put it back and re-wrap in its wrapper.

- Leftover cheese can be stored in the fridge. The best place is in the vegetable compartment where the atmosphere is the most humid and the fridge is warmest.

Serving Cheese

- Cheese boards should contain a balanced presentation of main types, usually no more than five cheeses, e.g. surface-ripened, white mould/washed rind, goat's cheese, hard cheese, blue cheese. Two or three specialty cheeses are better than half a dozen displayed just for effect. As cheese should be eaten in order of increasing flavour, arrange cheeses in a logical sequence. If there is a very strong cheese, avoid cross-tastes by providing two knives or serve on separate trays.

- Display cheese on a tray, preferably of natural materials, e.g. glass, wicker, wood, etc. If possible use leaves or straw mats between the cheese and the tray for added contrast.

- For accompaniments, provide good whole-grain bread or crackers, fresh fruit or herbs or spices that match the cheese, e.g. fresh herbs with goat's cheese, cumin with Munster. Unsalted butter should be available as a method of toning down strong cheese flavours.

- Remove unnecessary or difficult rinds if you wish, particularly on hard cheeses. As a general rule, the rinds of most cheeses are not eaten.

- Cheeses should be served at room temperature so remove from the fridge or store in a cupboard at least one hour prior to serving. It is a good idea to cover the cheese with a damp cloth while the meal is in progress.
- Cheese should only be served in quantities that can be eaten, as oscillations in temperature will destroy what is left over.
- Cheese is usually served between courses to prepare the palate after eating. Always eat cheese with wine or alcoholic beverages, never with water.

Cheese can cause stomach aches if eaten with water.

- Try and balance wine and cheeses and avoid conflict of tastes. Wine also needs to be balanced: the wines served should be at least as strong as the wines served with previous courses. There are no hard and fast combinations and personal taste is best. Generally the lighter the wine, the less aged the cheese. It is also interesting to try other local beverages with local cheeses, e.g. cider and camembert.

Bill Studd, Victoria

HERB AND CHEESE SOUFFLÉS WITH TOMATO-FLAVOURED SAUCE

60 g flour
1 cup cold milk
1 teaspoon Dijon mustard
3 egg yolks
1 teaspoon very finely chopped herbs
freshly ground pepper and nutmeg
4 egg whites
pinch salt
³/4 cup grated Gruyère cheese

SAUCE
1¹/2 cups thickened cream
6 teaspoons tomato concentrate
1 teaspoon finely chopped tarragon
freshly ground pepper and pinch salt

Butter 6 small soufflé moulds. Refrigerate and butter again. Sift the flour into a heavy-based saucepan. Stir in a little milk. Continue to add milk, stirring, until the mixture becomes a thick, smooth paste. Pour in the rest of the milk and mix thoroughly. Put the saucepan on a low heat and stir constantly until it begins to thicken. Remove the saucepan from the heat and beat hard. It lumps easily, so go back and forth to the heat until a thick, smooth paste is formed. Turn off the heat, add the mustard and egg yolks one at a time, beating well after each addition. Add the herbs, pepper and nutmeg. Set aside.

Beat the egg whites with the salt until thick. Fold a little egg white into the egg yolk base, then fold the base mixture with the egg whites using a spatula. Scatter ¹/2 cup of the cheese in at the last minute and spoon the mixture equally into the prepared moulds. Bake at 190°C in a bain-marie for about 15 minutes or until they have risen and are pale brown on top.

Butter a gratin dish large enough to hold the moulds. Remove the soufflés from the oven and gently tip them out of the moulds. Arrange them right side up in the gratin dish and pour on the sauce. Sprinkle the extra cheese on top. Bake the soufflés for a further 20 minutes or until they have swollen and are brown on top. Remove to hot serving plates with an egg slide.

Sauce: Heat all the ingredients in a saucepan and reduce to thicken slightly.

Penny Smith, Victoria

To keep cheese fresh, *place on a covered dish with a lump of sugar.*

FETTUCCINE CON QUATRO FORMAGGI
(Fettucine with Four Cheese Sauce)

RICHARD THOMAS writes:

The sounds of summer in northern Victoria are still the strongest memories of my years on our farm. Each one was harsh against the still, wilting, hot silence.

All the animals listless, retiring to the shade, escaping the foot-blistering heat. A crow's lazy progress, in search of carrion, calling its 'Warrrk!' The satisfied croak of a chook fluffing up in the dust from the bald earth under our peppercorn trees, which filled the air with stinging resin in the midday heat. The crack of Dad's axe into the stubborn redgum as he worked to keep the stove hot, then the rumble of wood into the woodbox at the back door. The tinny clamour of the truck as it clanked its way down the crushed rock road to collect the milk which stood in cans at the gate, the handles too hot for we kids to hold. Or cream, sometimes days old, thickening into clots.

And down in the dairy, the whirr of our separator, well oiled, sounding its bell at each revolution to let my father know if we were rushing or dreaming. 'Keep that speed up a bit,' he'd shout. 'Cream's getting a bit thin!' He'd know this without even seeing it. We never worked out how, at the time. Just one of those things grown-ups knew, we guessed.

Occasionally Mr Hamilton's Tiger Moth edged its way across our sky, droning, slower than a walk. The milk truck moved on erratically, towards Numurkah.

Years later I would learn to grade that cream into Choice, First and Reject—Choice with its clean sourness, still liquid, for export butter; First, often crusty and lumpy as it clotted; and Reject, ropey and ant-infested.

But the cream then made wonderful butter and the milk made even better cheese—milk already half-ripe, full of flavour-producing bacteria. Each bacteria gave its single cell of life to be digested, along with the fats and proteins in the cheeses, by succeeding generations of bacteria. They yielded warm, rich, rounded flavours within six months—enough flavour to shame the vintage cheeses of today.

Of course, the spring and summer milk gave the best cheeses—the luscious pasture grass, milk ripened by the sun. But what of autumn and winter? Grasses and ripeness stunted as puddles froze over. Cows, bad-tempered and unyielding, fed on mouldy hay. The milk had little to offer the cheesemaker. Then, in a flurry of 1960s technology, we got an electric fridge at home. No more smoky haze from a poorly tuned kero burner, freezing the eggs solid one day and thawing the ice-cream the next. Technology also gave us bulk milk tanks of stainless steel, with chillers. We kept ours gleaming, wiped every day with the leftover kero.

With feed concentrates for the cows, and milk kept ice-cold to preserve it, I saw, without knowing it, the death of seasonal cheese in this country. Pasteurisers, homogenisers and deodorisers all bring milk farm-fresh to our factory door, 365 days a year. Today I import cultures of exotic, flavour-producing bacteria, yeasts and moulds. These reintroduce flavour and character into the milk at cheesemaking.   ▶

SAUCE

90 g *Emmental cheese,
grated*
250 ml *carton crème fraîche
or sour cream*
60 g *fresh hard-grating
cheese, grated*
dash of brandy
90 g *soft blue cheese*
cracked black pepper

PASTA

90 g *each tomato, plain and
spinach fettuccine*

GARNISH

1 *small red pepper*
½ *cup fresh basil, shredded*

Toast the red pepper over a gas flame, wash off the blackened skin and slice finely.

In a heavy saucepan warm the grated Emmental to melting point. Add about a third of the crème fraîche, stirring slowly. When smooth, add the grating cheese and blend it in. Use more crème fraîche to thin the sauce if necessary. Cook the fettuccine and drain. Swirl in a knob of butter. Put the pasta into four colourful bowls. Just before serving the sauce, splash in the brandy and break in the blue cheese. Stir. Spoon the sauce over the pasta, sprinkle on a little black pepper, garnish with the red pepper and basil, and serve.

SERVES 4

Richard Thomas, Victoria

....

Cottage cheese *will remain fresher longer in the
refrigerator if it is stored upside-down.*

Freeze whole bunches of grapes *to use as a garnish,
or on a cheese platter. They are delicious straight from
the freezer or as a refresher in place of a sorbet.*

Lemons

.
.
.
.
.
.
.
.

FRESH LEMONADE

MUNGUMBY LODGE is a bush retreat at Helendale, 35 km from Cooktown, Queensland. Nick and Lizzie Marshall run this haven, built in the rainforest amongst dense tropical foliage, mango trees and tropical plants. Green lawns and a tended garden surround the guest cabins and lodge. It is a retreat for anyone interested in nature and tourists who wish to see Australian tropics at first hand in extremely comfortable conditions. Lizzie, an Irish girl, is a fine cook and she shared the following favourite with me.

'As we have a fantastic lemon tree in the middle of our garden, I am always looking for new ways to use up the lemons. This lemonade is a taste I remember from childhood. I was one of six girls and we always fought to stir in the sugar. It is an ideal drink for the tropics—cool and refreshing.'

juice and grated rind of
  3 lemons
25 g citric acid
450 g white sugar
1 litre boiling water

Mix all the ingredients together in a large bowl and pour on the boiling water. Stir well until the sugar has dissolved. Cool and refrigerate.

Lizzie Marshall, Far North Queensland

Add a couple of teaspoons of vinegar, *lemon juice or wine to the water when poaching eggs. They will not only hold their shape better but also taste better. Another way to make poached eggs hold their shape is to put the unbroken egg into a pot of boiling water for 10 seconds and then break it into the pan of poaching water.*

LEMON SYRUP

SARAH GUEST writes:

In my English childhood there were no lemon trees. We had an orchard and grew quite a variety of fruiting trees against the warmth of brick walls, but it was far too cold for citrus. I saw my first lemon tree on arrival in Australia when I was twenty and have been on about them ever since. The trees can be chopped without suffering too much harm. My pair have been given the form of low standards and have a somewhat formal, eighteenth-century air about them. The waxy, white flowers have a delicate charm and a heavenly scent. My Lisbon lemons are ideally suited to the domestic garden, carrying flowers and fruit and at the same time providing a year-round supply for the kitchen and the gin! All this domestic magic from the one tree. Why do people plant lemon trees in their back gardens? Does the rotary clothes hoist need company? I grow mine in the front where they provide a background of greenery in a small courtyard. I regularly hear visitors murmuring about my English eccentricity. If lemon trees were hard to grow, of course, it would be a different story.

A basketful of lemons to yield 625 ml (2½ cups) lemon juice
1.5 kg white sugar
375 ml (1½ cups) water
½ teaspoon tartaric acid
½ teaspoon citric acid

Wash the lemons and remove the zest. Put the zest, water and sugar into a large pan and stir over heat until the sugar has dissolved. Add the lemon juice and acids (which will help prolong the life of the brew), strain and bottle in glass. This syrup can be used as a cordial: dilute 1 part cordial to 4-5 parts water.

Sarah Guest, Victoria

Keep lemon halves *in your kitchen to remove odours from your refrigerator, to rub your nails with to remove stains, odour and dirt, and to add to rice while you are cooking or to potatoes while boiling.*

Add a little lemon juice *to potatoes when boiling to improve their colour.*

Wine

WINE & FOOD

WINE and most types of food are inseparable, but one of the most frequently asked questions is, 'What wine goes with which food?' Alas, there is no easy answer to this question.

Wine is like music—it can set the mood or it can drive you crazy. As with music, wine has a high fashion quotient, and the appreciation of both is a highly individual thing. You may not see the genius of the music of Thelonius Monk, and bagpipes might send me scurrying for the earplugs. The pan pipes of the Andes carry me away, but grand opera bores me rigid. So it is with wine styles —that's why there are no rules about matching wine and food.

The ancient wisdom was that dark meat went with red wine and white meat demanded white wine. Fine in theory, but try a beaujolais with gamey venison and you might as well drink water. Team a heavily wooded chardonnay with whiting and you may as well not eat at all. Clearly the roles of both wines could be reversed. The chardonnay could possibly handle the venison, but the beaujolais probably wouldn't suit the whiting. Beaujolais served with a blood fish like tuna can be quite a treat. It becomes a matter of matching the strength of flavour of the food with a similar-strength wine. Delicate food requires delicate wines and robust food requires the equivalent of the Ride of the Valkyries in the bottle.

It sounds simple, but there are traps for young and old players. Take curry, for example. There is no wine which can match a curry, but if you insist, the best wine is cheap wine, well chilled. You are not going to taste the stuff, so why waste the best in your cellar? The better bet is to team spicy food with beer or cider. They are cheap and they can extinguish the fires.

Another no man's land for wine is the realms of pickled foods. The nemesis of wine is vinegar—in fact if wine wears out its welcome it will become vinegar, so it is very unfair to ask it to team with acetic acid. Rollmops and rhine riesling simply don't go together. They resemble one of Thelonius Monk's more bizarre discords.

Another difficult area is that of salted food. What wine matches corned beef? The best way round that is to use the wine as the cooking medium. Poach your beef in, say, Cab Mac and you've got the answer—you serve Cab Mac. But common or garden boiled corned beef is pretty difficult to match because of the high salt content.

Smoked food can also be a worry. Delicate flavours like smoked trout are not a problem—a mature white burgundy style would probably work well. But what wine would you match with kippers? At a guess (and I'm not in a hurry to find out), I would nominate a good *flor fino* sherry which has been well chilled.

That brings us to the area of soup. Somehow it seems silly to want to serve liquid with liquid, but conventional wisdom dictates an amontillado sherry with a clear soup like consommé. If you must, you must...

At the other end of the meal, things like chocolate dessert cause problems. The only wine I've found to match rich chocolate is Rutherglen Tokay and that's after it's been stored in the refrigerator's freezer until it becomes viscous. This chilled delight works well with chocolate, but the unusual method of serving will cause winemakers to shake their heads.

That brings us to the idea of serving one type of wine exclusively throughout a meal. I've sat through many dinners where it has been tried and to my mind it just doesn't work. To quote an example, Bollinger hosted a very impressive dinner at which they served only champagne with the seven courses. They were beautiful champagnes and in some cases two or three wines were served in brackets. All in all, we had fourteen different champagnes, which was very generous and, you'd think, heavenly. Not so. I thought I had discovered a hitherto unknown peptic ulcer. The acid build-up was fantastic—I couldn't get at the antacid tablets fast enough. It was a case of too much of a good thing.

A similar thing happened at a dinner where sauternes were served exclusively. I know there is a school of thought that says this can be done and I've seen D'Yquem team well with smoked salmon and Beluga caviar, but on this occasion the procession of sauternes became very tedious, and in some cases the wine and food clashed. The whiting and lobster course was swamped by the wine, which was too highly flavoured for the delicate fare. And again it was too much of a good thing. Near the end of the meal I started to wonder whether I was a candidate for diabetes.

After many similar experiences, I've concluded that variety is the spice of life. Theme dinners can be dashed against the rocks of boredom—there is no substitute for a balanced range of wine and flavours. But saying that is somehow to set a rule and, as I said in the beginning, there are no rules.

There is no accounting for taste, either. If you like your Lafite with lemonade, so be it (and I know someone who does). The main thing is that you and your guests derive the most enjoyment from your food and wine. Perhaps that is achieved best by establishing balance and harmony. Combining like flavours and blending them into a harmonious chord—a chord as grand as those of Beethoven or as intricate as those of Mozart—is what it is all about. Then wine and food can be a marriage made in heaven.

Mark Shield, Victoria

HEDGEROW WINES
IN AUSTRALIA

IMAGINE WINE, or a drink very much like it, made from the fruit of the tamarillo, orange, plum, feijoa, a wide variety of beans, from lemon juice infused with herbs like thyme, mint or parsley, from rose petals, or from the more pedestrian carrot or potato. This is the world of home-made wine, or 'wine from the hedgerow' as it is sometimes known in Britain.

The question of what to call such beverages is a little vexing; my dictionary describes wine as the product of fermented fruit juice, especially grapes. This covers the ubiquitous backyard plum and the odd feijoa, but what of the grand old potato, the sweeter carrot and the like?

On a mild morning in the English spring of 1983 my wife Joan, son Leighton and I drove to the Greater London suburb of Ruislip to lunch with Ben Turner and his wife. Ben was a legendary figure and author in the field of amateur wine.

After a fine amontillado sherry, we settled down to a meal of roast beef, with which Ben served two masked wines. Apart from one or two guarded comments, Ben was poker-faced as he waited for me to comment on the character and pedigree of what was before me. I suggested that the wine on the left was made from grapes and the one on the right was not. Ben remained poker-faced. He pressed me further to state the variety and origin of the grape wine. I answered 'shiraz' and 'Australian', unable to be any more specific. Ben turned the conversation to the relative merits of the two wines. To my palate, both showed significant age. The shiraz (if that's what it was) offered obvious bottle maturity; there was some depth and complexity even though the wine was not great. The other wine lacked the weight of its mate but had more detailed fruit flavour and, in that, was more subtle in its complexity. After further consideration, Ben revealed the first wine to be a shiraz from Brands of Coonawarra and the second a plum wine from his own hand. Both were vintaged in 1972.

I asked him whether the products of the orchard, the vegetable patch and the hedgerow have the right to the term 'wine'. Ben left the room for a few seconds, returned with one of his books, *The Winemaker's Encyclopaedia*, and asked me to read the following passage:

'*The Shorter Oxford Dictionary* suggests that the word "wine" comes from the Old English win which came from the Latin *vinum*. In turn, it is thought probable that *vinum* or similar words such as the Greek *oinos* had a common Mediterranean source. Perhaps they were derived from the Sanskrit word *vena* which meant "drink offering". Such a *vena* was the Vedic Liquor, used as an essential part of ancient sacrificial offerings, that was made from the juice extracted from the plant Soma, by crushing it between two millstones. It became a "golden nectar, the drink of the gods". It was an ambrosia, supposed to defeat death for all who drank it, and symbolised immortality. It appears, however, that only the priests were allowed to drink it and not the worshippers. If this derivation of the word "wine" is accurate, then it is correctly used by the amateur winemaker of today.'

Having settled that question, we continued to ponder the two wines before us and ended a satisfying and informative day agreeing the plum had a slight edge.

Home-made wine has been a big industry in the British Isles for some time; the momentum fell away during the World Wars and then afterwards due to government controls on sugar. In the 1950s the number of Britons watching their fermenting elderberry was on the increase again. By the time we reached England in 1981, whole rows in major retail chains such as Boots were devoted to the wherewithal of amateur winemaking. Then, as now, it is considered a valid and inexpensive alternative to the commercial labels.

In Australia, home-made wine has never had the same hold. In the main, it has been pursued by those of European origin for whom making wine is part of the fabric of life. Much of the amateur wine is made from grapes purchased from the back of trucks at the major markets. Because the initial fruit quality is never better than fair, the resultant wine would struggle to satisfy those wine-lovers weaned on commercial product.

There are three or four amateur winemaking guilds in Victoria. I joined the Frankston Amateur Wine Guild in the late 1970s and have watched this enthusiastic group of 30 to 40 winemakers hone their techniques to the point where their feijoa, plum, ginger and kiwi fruit wines have matched the commercial standard. At its annual show, the Frankston Guild attracts more than 100 entries, the styles ranging from sparkling wines through to dry and sweeter table wines and on to stronger fare such as fortified cumquats.

The point about hedgerow wine is that it broadens the spectrum of sensation. The wines from grapes become one room in a mansion of flavour and complexity. This is not to downgrade the majesty of grape wine, rather its position is enhanced and given greater perspective against a more detailed background.

It is relatively easy to experience the delights of wine from the hedgerow: the step from interested bystander to participant is a small and inexpensive one. You need a supply of good-quality fruit or vegetables, a few other readily available ingredients, and some utensils. You need to spend an hour or so in preparation and then no more than ten minutes a day to monitor the results of your efforts.

Here is a recipe for plum wine, though the plums could be replaced by strawberries, raspberries, blackberries, pears, oranges, peaches, feijoas, tamarillos or many other fruits and vegetables. The recipe makes about $4^1/_2$ litres of plum wine. You will need a vessel in which to ferment the fruit and another in which to finish the fermentation. These can be purchased singly or as part of an amateur winemaking kit from specialist retailers like Australian Home Brewing in the Melbourne suburb of Hughesdale. They can also supply an appropriate yeast and other necessities. ▶

PLUM WINE

*about 4 kg plums, stones
    removed and finely
    chopped*
300 g raisins
2 litres water
2 kg sugar
a suitable cultured yeast
¼ tablespoon Pectonaze
¼ teaspoon nutrient salts
2 Campden tablets
½ teaspoon citric acid

Place the plums in the first vessel (a spotlessly clean bucket would do) along with the raisins, and pour the water over the mass. Add 750 g of the sugar, the yeast, Pectonaze, salts, Campden tablets and citric acid. Fermentation should start after 24 hours and the mixture will bubble away for 3 or 4 days before subsiding. Strain the fermenting juice and fruit through a piece of muslin or similar material (pantyhose can do the job admirably) into the second container (this time a 4.5 litre glass jar with a rubber-bung and airlock is necessary) and squeeze as much liquid from the retained pulp as you can. Add another 750 g of the sugar and top up with cooled boiled water to fill 80 per cent of the jar. After 10 days add the rest of the sugar. Under the airlock the juice will finish fermenting over a couple of weeks. At this point you could add a little extra sugar to taste.

Your new wine must be racked—a process where you siphon the wine off of any sediment that has fallen to the bottom of the vessel—at least twice, every three months or so, and allowed to mature. Throughout the entire process, cleanliness must be your catch-cry.

Six months after your initial effort, you will be able to offer a lightly sweet plum wine to your friends, as a chilled aperitif, in the balmy shade of an al fresco afternoon.

Robert Hicks, Victoria

A NOSE FOR ALL SEASONS

THE NOSE is all. We all have one and the proboscis capability is luckily not impaired by size. So no matter whether you've got a Jimmy Durante schnoz or a delicate Catherine Deneuve retroussé, the ability to have a computer-driven olfactory flavour program that combines a sense of smell and a memory bank is available to us all.

Wine stimulates all the senses, but the reality is that taste basically confirms the impressions set by sight and smell and adds to the sum total. Smell is the most basic and primitive of the senses. History shows that just as a label tells a great deal about a wine, sight assists smell. Many jokes have been played on great wine connoisseurs and indeed it is extremely difficult to nominate whether a wine is red or white, riesling or beaujolais, when sight is not allowed.

There are only a handful of tastes compared to the thousands of smells which pass across our nasal passages on a daily basis: for me, seasons are not only memorable for their colours and temperature variations but also most enjoyable for the aromas that are associated with them. The scent of summer jasmine flowers is as satisfying as those of the grasses and blossoms of spring.

To enjoy wine, and debate the worth of one wine against another, it is useful to develop a vocabulary of the smells that waft past your nostrils in daily life. This will avert the tendency to pomposity and encourage you to make a description in basic, everyday language. If a shiraz smells like a wet log-chopper's boot, then so be it! I have heard one noted Aussie wine judge describe a Grange Hermitage as raspberries, blackcurrants and boots, but he then redeemed himself by poetically describing Pewsey Vale Riesling as 'lifted, aromatic, delicate, scented, balanced, Fonteyn-like'.

The smell, brain or memory bank acts as an immediate catalyst of recognition and identification. The first impression is extremely valuable to the wine connoisseur, judge or experienced wine taster. Good wine will always smell good, clean, complex. Rarely ever have I tasted a good wine that smelled poorly. Some of the more pungent substances in wine have a physical impact that stimulates the nerve ending in a tactile sense.

Whether you are a professional, a mere quaffer or an interested child, everybody has a strong sense of smell. However the interested enthusiast will practise and learn more than the lesser practising drinker.

To give yourself a chance of getting the best out of a wine, start by selecting a decent wine glass. I've found the perfect glass is the XL5. It has a good-shaped bowl and a perfect-sized opening for both nosing and drinking.

When assessing wine, it is best to roll the wine round the glass gently and thereby cajole the tricky little esters out of the solution by aeration. (Esters, or flavour cells, are complex vapours that make up the aroma or bouquet of wine. 'Aroma' is the name given to the primary character of the grape variety, while 'bouquet' is the secondary or developed characters given by soil, region, oak, bottle maturity or winemaker.) This is a time of concentration on the various characters in the wine, and the brain short-circuits as we establish whether we can or should find blackcurrants, grapiness reminiscent of riesling or muscat, or the French way relating to flowers in the form of violets, daisies, roses, etc. The olfactory system processes all these complexities, involving along the way olfactory nerves, olfactory bulbs in the skull base, olfactory tracts (brain matter) and nerve cells which interpret the sensation.

I have always believed that first impressions are 90 per cent correct. This is the moment when you know whether your purchase has been a great find or a disaster. Naturally the characters should be positive and not bad odours.

After that process, one may ask, 'Is my brain capable of doing all that and still leaving enough time to drink?' We hope yes, but the enjoyment of wine is not confined to its ultimate consumption. I have lost count of the number of times that the joy of the lifted, rounded, sappy bouquet of great pinot noir or the cedary blackcurrant of cabernet sauvignon kept the wine from my lips for minutes on end.

Great wine takes time. Maybe the great pleasure of taste is merely the privilege of smell as a prior action. Indeed, we need a nose for all reasons. ▶

SOME SMELLS

Aroma/Bouquet

Positive Characters

Flowery:	Rhine riesling
Herbaceous/grassy:	Sauvignon blanc
Kerosene:	Old rhine riesling
Fig/melon:	Chardonnay
Spicy/haystack:	Traminer
Vanillin:	Often fresh oak character
Butterscotchy:	Older chardonnay
'Sweaty saddle':	Hunter Valley reds
Earthy:	McLaren Vale shiraz
Minty:	Often cabernet sauvignon
Bell-pepper:	Often syrah from California
Blackcurrant/cedar:	Cabernet
Peppery/spicy:	Syrah/shiraz from Rhône Valley and Coonawarra
Raisin:	Muscats from Rutherglen
Sappy/velvet:	Classic red burgundy

Negative Characters

Pungent, gassy:	Sulphur dioxide in excess
Rotten egg gas:	Hydrogen disulphide
Pickled, vinegary:	Acetic acid
Decaying, wet hessian:	Corked
Dank, bilgey:	Dirty wood
Porty:	Overripe red wine

Robert Hill Smith, South Australia

It is necessary *to cook and reduce wine in a pot before adding it to a sauce or casserole to volatise the alcohol and impart its delicious flavour.*

The hot sensation of curry *is further increased by the tannin in red wines. The sugar in a late-picked or semi-sweet white wine will reduce it.*

Soft, ripe, round wines *will accentuate fatty foods. A big, firmer, more tannic wine will cut through the fat, giving a balanced taste sensation.*

METRIC CONVERSION TABLES

VOLUME MEASURES

Imperial	Standard measures	Metric
$^1/_8$ fl oz	1 teaspoon	5 ml
$^1/_4$ fl oz	2 teaspoons	10 ml
$^1/_2$ fl oz	1 tablespoon	20 ml
1 fl oz	1$^1/_2$ tablespoons	30 ml
	2 tablespoons	40 ml
1$^1/_2$ fl oz	2$^1/_2$ tablespoons	50 ml
2 fl oz	3 tablespoons	60 ml
	$^1/_4$ cup	65 ml
	3$^1/_2$ tablespoons	70 ml
	4 tablespoons	80 ml
	$^1/_3$ cup	85 ml
	4$^1/_2$ tablespoons	90 ml
3 fl oz	5 tablespoons	100 ml
4 fl oz	$^1/_2$ cup	125 ml
5 fl oz ($^1/_4$ pint)	7$^1/_2$ tablespoons	150 ml
	$^2/_3$ cup	170 ml
6 fl oz	$^3/_4$ cup	185 ml
8 fl oz	1 cup	250 ml
10 fl oz ($^1/_2$ pint)	1$^1/_4$ cups	315 ml
12 fl oz	1$^1/_2$ cups	375 ml
14 fl oz	1$^3/_4$ cups	435 ml
16 fl oz	2 cups	500 ml
20 fl oz (1 pint)	2$^1/_2$ cups	625 ml
40 fl oz (1 quart)	5 cups	1.25 litres
80 fl oz ($^1/_2$ gallon)	10 cups	2.5 litres
120 fl oz ($^3/_4$ gallon)	15 cups	3.75 litres
160 fl oz (1 gallon)	20 cups	5.0 litres

WEIGHT MEASURES

Avoirdupois	Metric
$^1/_2$ oz	15 g
1 oz	30 g
2 oz	60 g
3 oz	90 g
4 oz ($^1/_4$ lb)	125 g
5 oz	155 g
6 oz	185 g
7 oz	220 g
8 oz ($^1/_2$ lb)	250 g
9 oz	280 g
10 oz	315 g
11 oz	345 g
12 oz ($^3/_4$ lb)	375 g
13 oz	410 g
14 oz	440 g
15 oz	470 g
16 oz (1 lb)	500 g (0.5 kg)
24 oz (1$^1/_2$ lb)	750 g
32 oz (2 lb)	1000 g (1 kg)
48 oz (3 lb)	1500 g (1.5 kg)
64 oz (4 lb)	2000 g (2 kg)

OVEN TEMPERATURES

Approximate Thermostat Setting °F (Fahrenheit)		Temperature Descriptions	Gas Mark	Approximate Thermostat Setting °C (Celsius)	
Gas	Electricity			Gas	Electricity
140	140	Plate warming	0	60	60
175	175	Keep warm	1/4	80	80
210	230	Cool	1/2	100	110
250	250	Very slow	1	120	120
300	300	Slow	2	150	150
320	340	Moderately slow	3	160	170
355	390	Moderate	4	180	200
375	430	Moderately hot	5	190	220
390	445	Hot	6	200	230
445	480	Very hot	7-8	230	250

WEIGHTS & MEASURES OF SHELLED NUTS

1 cup almonds	150 g
1 cup almond meal	120 g
1 cup cashews	140 g
1 cup chestnuts	125 g
1 cup desiccated coconut	70 g
1 cup hazelnuts	150 g
1 cup ground hazelnuts	125 g
1 cup macadamias	120 g
1 cup peanuts	150 g
1 cup pecans	120 g
1 cup ground pecans	100 g
1 cup pinenuts	120 g
1 cup pistachios	100 g
1 cup walnuts	120 g

INDEX